BIRTH ANGELS

Book of Days

Daily Wisdoms with the 72 Angels of the Tree of Life

Volume 3: August 17 ~ October 29

Relationship with Work and Purpose

Terah Cox

Stone's Throw Publishing House
August 2014

BIRTH ANGELS BOOK OF DAYS
Daily Wisdoms with the 72 Angels of the Tree of Life
Volume 3: August 17 ~ October 29
Relationship with Work and Purpose

Series includes:
Volume 1: March 21 – June 2
Relationship with the Divine
Volume 2: June 3 – August 16
Relationship with Self
Volume 3: August 17 – October 29
Relationship with Work and Purpose
Volume 4: October 30 – January 8
Relationship with Others
Volume 5: January 9 – March 20
Relationship with Community and the World

Stone's Throw Publishing House
ISBN-13: 978-0692293683
ISBN-10: 069229368X
First Edition Softcover | Volume 3: August 2014
Kindle Digital Edition | Volume 3: August 2014

For permissions, information about author
and additional books and materials, see
www.terahcox.com
www.heavenandearthworks.com

Book design by Terah Cox
Wing detail of Fresco Angel by Giotto di Bondone,
  Scenes from the Life of Christ #4 (1304-06)

Other Books by Terah Cox

BIRTH ANGELS BOOK OF DAYS ~ Vols. 1, 2
Daily Wisdoms with the 72 Angels of the Tree of Life
Stone's Throw Publishing House (March & May, 2014)

THE STORY OF LOVE & TRUTH
Stone's Throw Publishing House
Limited Handmade Edition (2007)
Illustrated Softcover Edition (2011)

BIRTH ANGELS ~ Fulfilling Your Life Purpose
with the 72 Angels of the Kabbalah
Andrews McMeel/Simon & Schuster (2004)
(acquired by Stone's Throw Publishing House 2013)
Greek edition: Asimakis Publishing, Athens, Greece (2014)
Czech edition: Barevny Svet s.r.o (2015)

YOU CAN WRITE SONG LYRICS
Writers Digest / F&W Publications (2001)

For permissions or information about author:
www.terahcox.com

Table of Contents

Gratitudes

During the now year-long journey of bringing forth the first three volumes of the BOOK OF DAYS series, I am so grateful for friends, family and extended family who have continued their encouragement, support and understanding – my nieces Hannah and Bekah and goddaughters Sara and Lindy, who I often draw upon for inspiration, along with their parents Art and Stacy and my sisters Connie and Cindy. Special gratitude to the soul-friends who have been spiritual companions and "visible other" counterparts to my inner muses – Stacie Florer, Jodi Tomasso, Amy Zachary, Lindy Labriola, Arnie Roman and Tanya Leah, Chuck Pisa, Teri Barr and Teresa Peppard. Our co-creative conversations have sparked lively explorations of ideas and expanded awarenesses in ways that only happen "when two or more are gathered" in like-heart-and-mindedness. Extra top-of-my-heart thanks to Stacie, Jodi, Amy and Lindy for reviewing much of the *Book of Days* materials and for your invaluable contributions, perspectives and insights as you have worked with the Angelic Energies and their wisdoms. Deep appreciation also to good friends and supporters Paula Mooney, Lesley Majzlin, the Delzells, Honey Kirila, Davina Long, Paxton McAbee, Cathleen O'Connor, Saskia Shakin, Barbara Lane, Dave Robbins, Jonathan & Cathie Robbins, Dominic Petrillo, Gittel Price, Rakesh Samani, Ellie Kimmelmam and Elizabeth Hepburn.

I also thank everyone who pre-ordered this volume for your cheerful patience in receiving it! When I realized the release would be late due to personal and professional urgencies, you have kindly allowed me to send the daily wisdoms via email until the actual book was released – and I thank you for your many positive messages appreciating the timely relevance of the wisdoms to your day's events and concerns. Stacie coalesced the feedback when she said it was like being part of the "real-time" publication of the book and the sense of participating in the process by receiving it "hot off the press." I also found that feeling the presence of real-time readers gave me a sense of intimacy with you all and heightened my sensitivity to the material itself as I was finishing up. Thank you for your encouragement and willingness to go with the flow and support the process! I'm so appreciative for all of you and the growing family of seekers and finders who have supported the *Birth Angels Book of Days* project with your reviews, patronage, encouragement, word-of-mouth, and more...

Aletheia Mystea, Amy Zachary, Anna Fyssa, Annie Lowe, Annie Shaw, Arnie Roman & Tanya Leah, Aura-Soma Koh, Barbara Lane, Beth Askew, Bobbie Martin, Bowie Yapp, Cathleen O'Connor, Chuck Pisa, Cindy Cox, Claudia Duchene, "Color Diva," Connie Kelley, Cornelius Chan, Crystal Yeung Kin Oi, Dana Ott, Darren Curtis, Dionissia Kapa, Dominic Petrillo, Dorothy Barr, Dorothy Trottier, Efi Konida, Eleonora Kouvoutsaki, Elizabeth Hepburn, Ephrem Holdener, Everr Phoenix, Fan Michail Anurag, Fedra Tsiaka, Fai-Wen Voon, Garie Lo, Gigi Lee, "Golden King," Harlina Aman, Hazel Ismail, Hazel, Yiu, Holly Koncz, Honey Kirila, Hung Chan, Katerina Palamidi, Imogene Drummond, Ishida Hiromi, Isobel Stamford, Jane Northup, Janice Tuchinsky, Jean Marzollo, Jeeval Kavassila, Jen Aly, Jenny Lou Murphy, Jodi Tomasso, Joyce Byrum, Judith Clements, Julie Ho, Karin Meury, Kaya & Christiane Muller, Kerry-Fleur Schleifer, Koya Yuen, Leiola Reeder, Lenka Markova, Liliana Fantina, Lili Tan, Liliana Fantini, Lim Tet Soon, Lindy Labriola, Liz Sugg, Lokita Ghirarduzzi, Loretta Melancon, Lorraine Bordiuk, Lulu Bouchard, Marc Sabin, Maria Macias, Mary Carolyn Lawson, Margrit Hugi, Maria Crisci, Maria Morana, Mary Gracely, Michelle Wong, Miho Aladiah, Mike Booth, Ming Oi Go, Patty Harpenau, Paula Mooney, Pauline Lum, Pauline Van Oirschot, Rebecca Mitchell, Renata Cherestes, Rita Dulaney, Sara Labriola, Saskia Shakin, Sarah Gallant, Shaleena MoonsStar, Sharon Etienne, Siew Teng Lee, Sook Kheng, Stacie & Shayne Florer, Stacy & Art Labriola, Stephanie Delzell, Stephanie Sulger, Sue Heiferman, Tanya Leah, Teresa Peppard, Tina Wettengel, Tracey Robertson, Ulrike Lauber, Vassiliki Filippou, Vivian Wong, Wendy Cheng, Yokow XhN, Yvonne Foo, Yuta Kubareva.

Eternal gratitude from the "grail-cauldron" of my heart to yours!

~ Terah, August 2014

Preface

This year-long co-creation between the "seen and unseen" worlds has shown me more than ever how much I, the work itself, and all beings and creations are ongoing works-in-progress – and that our time here is truly more about journeying than arriving. In realizing that the *Book of Days* needed to emerge over the year through five different volumes, I chose a publishing format that would give it the flexibility, time and space for it to become what it wants to be – and allow it to grow as my own clarity and consciousness grow. Every day of its way out into the world through my own within, I learn about the work and I learn about myself, and we both deepen. And all along the way, the felt presences of those who are supporting and participating in the project have added a beautiful dimension of co-experience to the continual birthing.

Thus, as with all who desire to express the love and truth of ourselves in the world, this work does not come to you written in stone. It comes as something fluid and with great feeling, hoping to help soften and reshape the hard things in our inner-outer lives, and to give us a breath of the eternal so that we may weather more gently time's tides of ebb and flow.

So let us have no regrets, only opportunities for more learning. And may every new today offer us wings for our journey and new horizons for our opening hearts.

Love and Light,

Terah, August 2014

TERAH COX

* * *

When you remember what you love,
you will know who you are.
When you know who you are,
you will know what to do.

And so...

Whenever the world
makes you forget the truth of yourself,
It is your purpose, the thing you love
that will bring you back,
again and again.

Introduction
Mining our Inner Gold

This third volume of the **Book of Days** features daily wisdoms with the 72 Angels about our relationship with work and purpose. As the Angelic Energies convey through their 72 different *angles* of light consciousness, work and purpose are not always the same thing. We can have many jobs and job titles in our lives, working for others or in our own enterprises and endeavors – but it is only when we are engaged in a way that exercises or at least points us in the direction of who we truly are and what we love – that our work *is* our purpose. The wisdoms suggest we can go at it in two broad ways: we can "work our purpose, or purpose our work." We can create or find work that directly exercises our purpose, or we can bring meaning and purpose to any kind of work through *why* and *how* we work. However we uniquely do it, a sense of purpose is vital to our aliveness and our individuation. And that's what we are here to do – to become more and more the unique individual that we each are – and thus have a true treasure and inspiration of beingness to offer others.

Despite tendencies to assess our own and each other's value by job title, income, address, possessions, fame or notoriety, deeds and works – to be a worthy component of the whole is registered in the soul using very different criteria. First, are we true to who we are in our heart of hearts? And secondly, are we bringing love, healing and helping to ourselves and others throughout the details and choices of our lives at every level? These inner criteria can take a whole lifetime to cultivate because they are not always our conscious focus. Often they are underlying more immediate worldly concerns – like needing to pay the rent and other bills, dealing with life's various detours, delays, challenges and changes, getting ourselves or kids through school, and so on.

As I have worked throughout this year on the *Book of Days* project, more and more has been brought into my consciousness about what we are doing here on this "privilege of Earth." The wisdoms say that our souls are as "outposts" of the Divine within humanity to give both the Divine and the Human an experience of life that can only happen on Earth through and because of our commingled Divine-Human beingness. In understanding our heart as the broadcaster of the Divine spark of Love and Truth that our soul carries, we can fathom that it is the unique dynamics of this love and truth within us that enlivens our physicality and gives our lives particular meaning and purpose. And that by and through our own meaning and purpose the co-creative power of love and truth are expanded and evolved throughout time and eternity, here on Earth and in all the universes.

It is has taken me a long time to even begin to understand the significance of love and truth in our lives. These are both grand and intimate concepts, and there has been much distortion of them through the ages by religions and personal and popular belief systems, as well as in our day-to-day personal lives. While love and truth are ideals we hold, both are as skewered in practice as they are idealized in theory. Everyone wants love, and the many different forms (or pantomimes) of it seem to be available to us in one way or another. But oddly, there are lots of claims to there being only one truth, and lots of people and groups claiming to have possession of that "only one truth!" From the time I was a kid questing after truth in everything and everyone, it always seemed more right to me that we each hold a piece of truth.

What I have been given inwardly to understand through my own spiritual sojourning, which has been filled in more deeply with the Angel wisdoms, is that in life, Truth is both **absolute** and **relative**. The Absolute Truth is the Divine "I AM," the pervasive universal constant of Oneness and Unity from and within which all of Creation proceeds and exists. "In the beginning," when the Oneness/Absolute Truth began to differentiate itself into physical existence as created things and beings, The I AMness of Truth was multiplied into relative aspects of Itself (that's us!). And so, here we each are – an individualized "isness" within the greater I AM, focalizing and expressing certain qualities of It in the physical as a relative rendering of Absolute Truth. Paradoxically, the wisdoms say, we also carry in our souls a "hologram," a sort of "tincture" of the Absolute, which continually informs and supports our individual/relative beingness and potential.

But to back up a little – for Truth to be initially multiplied and carried "abroad," something else was needed. That's where Love comes in. **Love** is the way Truth's I-AMness is ever evolving and expanding from the Divine into Creation. Through Love, Creation was, and continues to be, possible. Because of Love, the cosmos moves and expands. With Love, the wholeness of Truth can be revealed and known. Put in another way, you could think of Truth as a cosmic noun, and Love as the verb that expands and reveals it. But in their commingled state, they constitute all parts of "Divine creation speech," so to speak!

Thus in human life, **love is the creation energy which dwells within us to reveal and magnify the truth of**

who we are through the expression of our own soul-purposes and creations, and our healing and helping of others. Therefore, the love and truth that we each intrinsically are is derivative and expressive of the greater Love and Truth that compose the warp and woof of the All, the Whole, the Source-tapestry that is the template for physical life, and of which our souls are each a golden light-thread of commingled love-and-truthness. This is how we are created "in the image and likeness of the Divine."

All this cosmic information is carried within our souls and broadcast into our hearts as our personal truths, longings, enthusiasms, "inner tuitions" and wisdoms. Thus, while it is the nature of matter's density to muffle our soul memories and pull our consciousness into the physical, we can't help but feel a nagging emptiness unless we access our deeper inner resources which give meaning and purpose to our lives, our actions and our matter. And we cannot help but try to fill that emptiness, because it is the nature of life to want to be full and for love and truth to take root in creation. That is why we have an innate desire to seek, manifest and express more and more of who we are through our own evolving beingness, relationships and creations. And that is why when we have difficulty doing that, we resort to other less healthy "fillers." But there is a Divine lifeline dangling in our hearts that we often do not see until we are at the end of our own rope.

The 72 Angels tradition says that because we can so easily forget our indwelling Divine in the denser vibrations of our humanity, we have been given the gift of the Angels as "angles" of Divine Light and Consciousness – the "edible fruits of the Tree of Life" by which our inner Divine qualities may be nourished and disseminated into our human parts. Through our inner Divine we may come to know and grow into the greatness of who we are and what more we are capable of – just as the Divine Itself may come to know what more it can be through the expansion of itself within each of us and our own creations.

The more we understand that our lives are a co-creation between our Divine and Human parts, between our inner and outer aspects, our personal purpose and professional work, and in the interconnectedness of hearts near and far – only then will we be able to experience the magnitude of our potential to bear magnificent fruit and release truly nourishing and life-giving seeds for coming generations.

* * *

If you seek the thing you love
and love the thing you seek,
when you find it
it will find you back.

The Art of Individuation

Individuation is essentially about **increasing the truth of who we are by how we love**. There are as many individual, or relative, truths as there are beings and their creations, and as many ways to love as there are hearts, souls, minds and bodies doing it. Broadly, the ways in which we practice how we love and express our truths are through **our relationships with self and others and our work**. As the Angel wisdoms illuminate again and again, it seems to come down to not as much *who* we love as *how* we love, and not just *what* we do but *why* and *how* we do it. In every case, our best shot in loving well and being who we truly are is with wholeheartedness – indeed whole-beingness!

Being an individual means that we are "indivisible." We cannot be divided into separate parts because it takes all our parts to compose and sustain the whole that we are. Nevertheless, we treat the different aspects of ourselves and our multi-tasking lives with separate-consciousness every day. A pervasive example is the western model of specialized medicine that treats one part of the body without considering the whole being. Another is the different value systems we often have for different parts of our lives – one set of values for our loved ones, another for ourselves, another for our work-life, and yet another for the "them" that is the rest of the world. In all we do we are dividing ourselves and each other into seemingly unrelated parts! But as the Angel HABUHIAH says, *"...the boxes will inevitably leak into each other because in the underlying reality of unity, everything is a part, a reflection and a cause and effect of everything else."*

The ultimate key to a healthy relationship among the parts and the whole is perhaps modeled by the way holistic medicine works. The holistic approach knows that symptoms are pointers to what needs healing, which may be in a different part of the body than where the symptom is manifesting. Thus the whole being is treated – for even though some medicines and medical procedures can be a catalyst for healing, it is the integrity and power of the balanced whole that will ultimately heal the part that is sick.

How this translates to our work and purpose is in this way: if we choose work that is antagonistic to our true values, sense of meaning, purpose and well-being, then that part of our lives will become less and less supported by the whole of who we are, even cut off and compartmentalized – much in the same way that the body's internal defenses try to isolate disease within us to keep it from contaminating our whole being. However, if the "dis-ease" of our work-life goes on for too long, inner and outer conflict begins to occur – creating stress, dissension, divisiveness, a sense of emptiness, lethargy, and so on, until over time both our work and all other parts of our lives become weakened. Therefore, using the holistic model, we must treat the separated part by bringing it back into a wholeness-consciousness. On a practical level this means that we must either infuse compatible meaning into our work, or change our work so that it reflects the whole of who we truly are and what we need for well-being and the expressions of our love, meaning and purpose.

One of the keys to all this is understanding what our particular purpose is.

Seeking and Finding Purpose

The Angel wisdoms tell us that everyone's purpose in life shares a sameness in one fundamental three-part aspect, but has a total uniqueness in what we each do with those aspects. The sameness is that **our souls come to Earth to root and grow particular qualities of the Divine essence in human beingness so that (1) the Divine may have human experience and expression, (2) we may have a more enhanced and empowered experience of being human that is beyond the limitations of physical matter**, and that **(3) we may ultimately re-discover and express the underlying unity of which we all are part through the sameness of hearts beneath our seeming differences**.

What a beautiful win-win-win paradox! So while we are collectively here on Earth as an infinite multitude of diverse and unique Divine-Human beings, our individual purposes are to express and increase our own one-of-a-kind constellations of love-and-truth attributes, preferences and purposes, in ways that can only happen on Earth. In doing so, we elevate the physical matter of ourselves and our creations by becoming conscious and expressive of our Oneness within the context of seeming separateness.

Cultivating and expressing our individual purpose, or purposes, is one of the ways we individuate and contribute to the realization of Oneness. And the key to knowing the details of our particular purpose – what we are here to uniquely do and create – is to **become aware of what has resonance and meaning for us through what we have feeling, enthusiasm and passion for. In short, what we love.** Here in our heart of hearts, where our soul-truth has

9

implanted its purpose, lies our own personal field of dreams from which everything true and good in our lives can blossom. For when we know what we love, we can begin to know who we are. As scholar-mystic Stephen Cope says in his wonderful book about the realization and dynamics of life purpose, *The Greatest Work of Your Life* (Bantam Books, 2012), "in remembering who we really are, we are liberated from our striving to be somewhere else, someone else…[liberated] from both the past—our over-identification with past experiences of form—and from the future, our hopes and fears about future forms." (p. 208). Thus, in knowing who we are – in a way that is authentic and free from all idealizations, rationalizations and prescriptions from "the land of should," we can know what to do with our lives. And then, when the cacophony of the world sometimes makes us forget who we are, returning to what we love can bring us back to ourselves.

The distinctions of love, purpose and work. When all of these aspects are harmonious and supporting each other, they seem to become the same thing. However, I've presented them in this order for a reason. As long as each thing begets the next, starting with love, then you're in sync – your **love** fuels your **purpose** to express that love, which then becomes the **work** you do – or the way you do it. It is when your work – the outer, manifested expression of your love – takes on a kind of empty or dissatisfied feeling, that you know something is askew and needs refining or changing in the relationship between what you love and how you purpose it.

Over time we can confuse the action of our doing with the love and purpose behind the action and think it's the action that is the purpose. As we continue along in that action, or work, there may come a time when the work is not as interesting, or even available, to us. And if we've confused the meaning behind the action with the action itself, we can spin off into an existential, self-identification crisis that confuses work with self-worth and who we even are, etc. – when what's likely happening is just that what we love is wanting to grow into a new way and where of working.

For example, let's say you're an artist who loves to paint flowers, and you work for a catalog company doing just that. Suddenly one day, the company is sold and the new owners decide they want photographs of flowers rather than paintings, so you're about to lose your job since you're a painter, not a photographer – or that's how you identify yourself anyway. Suddenly you're not "good enough." And so here is where self-identification with the *action* of your work can have you defeatedly looking for another job – or – you can use the change in the job description as an opportunity to grow what you love – whether you stay or leave. To do that, you must return to the love that first purposed your work.

If you realize that as much as you enjoy painting, what you truly love are the flowers themselves, and painting them has just been the way your love purposed, or expressed, itself. Then you will realize there are other ways to explore and express your love – such as through a camera lens. And suddenly that seems exciting! So you ask the new owners to let you make the transition. They decide to give you a shot – and you come to love it! Then one day you are inspired to incorporate some painting elements with the photography, and that further inspires you to create a line of prints and cards. And then the catalog company features your work as a new product, and it becomes so successful that you ultimately leave the company and start a whole line of products with your unique multi-media floral imaging. How wonderful! Your own company and all of those actions and products are the new and expanded ways you have purposed what you love. But – if your company does not succeed, or another company makes you an offer you can't refuse, you will still have your love and all the ways it has grown – and you can re-form and repurpose it again. And if you dig deeper to understand why you love flowers – perhaps because they represent an unadulterated beauty – you may even branch out into trees, sunsets and so much more!

In summary, clarifying for ourselves the distinctions between the love that fuels our purpose, and the work that gives our purpose time and place, helps our greatest asset – what we love – to survive the fluctuations of ebb and flow in the outer world. Thus, when our work changes or goes away, our love can rise up out of the ashes of its previous form to create a new form and a new way and place to grow and express itself.

When purpose is hiding in plain sight. My own journey of *putting my love to work* was a long and winding road to the treasure that was always already here. As a kid with a lot of home-challenges, reading took me into other worlds and ways of being, and that instilled in me a wonder for words – not only how the words could open my eyes and heart and make me feel and aspire to things, but especially how words and feelings would reveal underlying truths in myself and others that seemed to be connected to "the better" in us. Feeling and listening became my ways of accessing those truths, and writing a way to give them form. So what to do with all that?

Even though I was always writing, it never occurred to me to BE a writer. I think it was because for a long time the writing itself was incidental to the inner experiences I was having with the meanings and energies of the words, which were my gates to the unknown and the truths I sought. I thought, however, because I loved words and literature and inspiring others, that I might become a teacher. But after a college degree in literature without teaching credentials, I veered off into fashion design and textiles (my other loves of color and fabric). Still, I was always sneaking into bathrooms and taking longer lunch hours to write. And when I saw that my colleagues in fashion were all having more success than me, I realized that the difference between us was that they loved what they were doing, and I didn't. I remember that day of realization, while sitting in a coffee shop writing on my lunch hour, that I would never excel at anything unless I loved it enough to keep doing it even if life gave me every reason not to. And then I realized that the only thing I loved that much was writing poetry, and it occurred to me I could teach it as a way of earning a living. So I left the fashion industry and was halfway through a masters in "poetics" when I realized that I didn't want to teach or critique it, I wanted to do it – but in some different way. So I took my love of words and put them to music and became a songwriter.

By that time my family thought I was a total flake – until I got my first contract with a major film company as a staff lyric writer, and suddenly I was a professional. Twenty years and 1000 or so songs later, I started to feel that I needed more than 3-1/2 minutes to say all that I wanted to say, and in a voice that was my own. It was hard to walk away from a career and community of friends I had worked with for years, but when I hit certain pinnacles of success and still felt empty, the writing was on the wall, so to speak. On a day when I returned from Europe, having co-written an entire album and numerous other songs with recording artists there, I put my bags down and walked up into the mountain forest across from my house to face the change I knew had to come. Halfway up, I tripped over a stone embedded in the path and looked down to see the perfect shape of a cleft heart. Just then an inner voice said to me, "if you follow your heart your feet will know where to go." I realized that I didn't know where my heart was anymore, and so I walked around and around that mountain path until I found it again.

On that day I finally remembered that my love of writing was about the "why" of writing – because the inspirations that came to me while writing gave me access to what I secretly really loved and had always loved – truth itself. Many of the songs and poems I had written through the years flashed before me in that moment, and I saw how I was always trying to get to the truth of an emotion, a feeling, an idea, a person. For me, a poem or any piece of writing wasn't authentic unless it sought something true and dared to find it. In that moment I let go of my songwriter-identification, and soon started writing my first book. In the usual way of beginner's luck, I got a book deal from a major publisher soon after and the book sold out two editions. Then of course, it all got harder – just when I was too far along my new path to turn back! Right after 9/11, I made another big shift, as many people in New York did at that time. I started writing poetry again and brought back my love of color and design by creating my own line of greeting cards and framed poetry-art, which began to support my "serious" goals of writing books, conducting workshops and coaching.

So I have come to realize that while I have done many kinds of work, there has been a golden thread of the same love – the love of truth – giving purpose to whatever work I was doing. But there was more. Ultimately, my love of truth has taught me about love itself, illuminating for me a greater truth about truth, which is that *any truth without love is not a whole truth.* Just as you or I or any of us will not discover the whole truth of who we are and what we are here for without the love that lives inside us – the love that is the creation energy which brought us into being and continues to sustain us – the love that tells the greater truth about anything or anyone we may think we know. And so now, my love has grown to include the love of love and truth both! But still, there's something more.

Understanding why you love what you love. We most often identify what we love by the "what" of it, rather than the "why." But that which you love needs your why to be conscious, because that why is connected to its very nature, which wants to be known. Such as when someone tells you they love you, and you feel to ask, "why?" And you're probably not wanting to hear platitudes about how much you've done for them – but rather something that shows they know and appreciate who you uniquely are in and of yourself.

Just as with the visible others in your life, you are also in relationship with the invisible others inside you – the holy ones of the Divine, the Angels, the inner muses who contribute, if you allow them, to everything you are and create in the visible world. Come to know them and you will better know yourself. Co-create with them and your creations will have power and purpose that reflects not only who you are but what more you long to be. Love them, and they will, together with you, help to love the magnificent totality of you into being. Thereby you will meet the why of your soul in the fullness of earthly purpose.

The person who loves to paint will need to realize the deeper why of her love if one day she can no longer do the physical work of painting. Athletes who have suffered debilitating injuries often have to repurpose not only what they loved about playing, but what they love about living. Some become coaches, motivational speakers, authors, counselors, inventors and so on, while others imbue their seeming impairment with so much love and determination that they are able to create a new agility or skill and participate in their sport in a whole new way. Bethany Hamilton, the young surfer girl whose arm was bitten off by a shark, learned how to handle her board and her balance differently and surf competitively with one arm. Amy Palmiero-Winters, a long-distance competitive runner who after an accident and amputation learned to run with one prosthetic leg, went on to win at least 11 world records. Actor Christopher Reeve, of *Superman* fame, repurposed his life to become an inspiring speaker and charitable force in the world after a horse-riding accident that left him paralyzed from the neck down. Injured soldiers, with both visible and invisible wounds, have especially difficult challenges in re-creating their lives at every level after combat, and those who leave active service are often starting over in repurposing their lives.

Whatever we may face, we are usually stronger than we know until we have to call on those hidden strengths to find our way back again – the most powerful being our willingness to love, howevermuch that may have receded for a time because of work demands, actions or circumstances. It is never too late to reconnect with heart and soul to revive the love within us so that we may create new and even unexpected ways of being and doing.

In finally going deeper in to ask myself what I love about love and truth, I realized the greater underlying love that those two loves has enabled me to experience, which author-poet Mark Nepo put so simply and beautifully in an Oprah interview. He said there was a time when "I had to put aside my identification with being a poet, and even the poem itself – so that I could fall in love again with the Spirit that gave me the poetry."

Here in our hearts, at the innermost altar of our love, beyond words and form, is where we meet the Source of our inspiration, the I Am of Love itself, which knows the whole Truth and Worth of who we are and what we love. This is what is at the core of everything we lovingly create – the "in-spiriting" of Truth's creation energy of Love that activates the love and truth within our own hearts. With this we are given the greater seeing, feeling and knowing that enables us to create works and lives that inspire love and truth and the living presence of that Spirit in the hearts of others.

When your love seems too ordinary. Sometimes we are doing our purpose all along and do not realize it for the dreaming of a seeming grander purpose. A children's book which captures this so beautifully, *Miss Rumphius* (by Barbara Cooney, Viking Books 1982), is based on a real-life woman by that name whose legacy of love and purpose still lives on today.

When Miss Rumphius was a little girl, she told her grandfather that when she was grown up she would go to faraway places, and then come back to live by the sea when she was old. He told her she must do a third thing in her life, "You must do something to make the world more beautiful." Miss Rumphius grew up and indeed traveled far and wide, and then moved to Maine to live in a house by the sea. She remembered the third thing she was supposed to do, but there was already so much beauty around her. She planted a few seeds around her house, and then she got back trouble and became bedridden for some time. A few months later, out her window she could see the blue and purple and rose-colored lupines she had planted and wished she could plant more. But she wasn't able to. A year or so later on a warm Spring day she finally felt well enough to walk about again, so she left her house to head toward the village. And then she saw on the other side of the hill a large patch of lupine flowers. "It was the wind that brought the seeds from my garden here! And the birds must have helped them!" she exclaimed. And so, from then on, wherever she walked, along the paths and across the fields and near the sand dunes, she scattered seeds. And next Spring there were tall beautiful blue and purple and rose-colored lupine flowers everywhere. And she understood that her third purpose in life, to make the world more beautiful, had been realized.

There are so many people living seemingly ordinary lives, doing seemingly ordinary things without noticeable public impact or accolades – but they are making a difference one smile and kind word at a time, one moment and day of loving and appreciating and helping to the next. There is nothing more sacred and important than that. Imagine knowing your purpose is just to scatter the seeds of your particular inner treasures wherever you go. And to not need them to be better than anyone else's, but just the best of yourself in that moment. And to not stand over them to make sure they yield what you or the world thinks they should, because you finally realize it's not all up to you to do it all, for time and the eternal and all beings, seen and unseen, are your co-creators.

When you have forgotten what you love. Of all the quandaries and conflicts I've encountered with people seeking their purpose, those who suffer most seem to be the ones who have forgotten what they love or put it totally out of their conscious realm in terms of doability. Thus they stay in jobs that make them miserable, depressed or even sick because they don't know what else to do. The wisdom of JELIEL says, if you don't know what to do with your life, *"then you have likely forgotten what you love or that working at what you love is even an option. And it may be you forgot because you decided at some point that what you loved wouldn't love you back, wouldn't get you other things you wanted, or that it wouldn't have financially practical or lasting value in your world. Thus you put your heart's desire 'out of mind' so as not to live with the longing or pain of abandoning the truth of yourself."* When this happens, we become stuck between a rock of our own resistance and a hard place of self-judgment.

I have seen again and again that when I don't know what to do about something, it's because I'm weighing all the options my brain can access, but nothing I can think of gives me an answer. This is why: The brain is like a computer with a lot of downloading, processing and data storage going on. It can only offer us the facts of what we already know or continue to accumulate. When we are facing any decision with indecisiveness, it is usually because we haven't consulted our heart – and the powers of "quantum knowing," as in intuition, and the conjuring of potential that is the heart's sole realm. Your mind doesn't have a clue what your purpose is –

that's your heart's job, because only your heart knows what you love. And it's only when your heart lets your mind know what that is, that then your mind and the rest of your parts can help you get there.

So the first step in figuring out your purpose at any point in your life is to (1) **embrace as a personal truth that what you love is of utmost, bottom-line, top-drawer importance to the quality and purpose of your life and being**; then (2) **let that love out of the closet**.

The hardest thing in life to do is to remember a love that we have pushed down, aside, back, away – because we have usually stacked a whole lot of stuff on top it, and ourselves, so as not to feel that pain or longing of separation. This is for sure: to find your purpose in life, you've got to bring that love back from behind everything else and up to the surface. If what you once loved is so far back in your closet that it seems it will never be findable again, I suggest to start cleaning out of your closet everything that's standing between you and it. That depth of excavation can involve past, present and future ideas of who you or someone else may have thought or still thinks you should be. It may also involve separating what you might want from any assumptions of impossibility – remembering that possibility is the comfortable realm of mind, and impossibility that of heart and its power of quantum leaping. It may be difficult, but it's not impossible – as long as you are using your heart as a shovel!

It can help to let your heart-memories take you back to things you loved to do as a kid without even thinking – and certainly before you ever considered the practicality of them! Somewhere in the seeds of childhood, even those fraught with adversity or abuse, our talents and gifts are there, shining like shards of light as our saving graces and clues to who we are. You may also find in your closet a whole bunch of practical reasons standing between you and what you love. If you have to support yourself, and perhaps other loved ones, it will involve examining what support, and happiness, really mean to you – are they based on acquisitional or existential criteria? In other words, does being able to buy things make you happier than being and doing who you are and spending time with the ones you love?

I have heard numerous stories of families who realized that their lives were being totally run by their monthly financial and lifestyle demands – until they decided to "sell it all" and go live somewhere that would allow them more time and opportunity to be together and do things they really enjoyed. One family of five sold everything they had to finance their tour around the world for a few years to help poorer areas build schools and homes, irrigate and farm and do whatever needed doing. While they were certainly doing a lot of great things for other people, the family itself, including the kids, felt that the best part of their experiences was that they got to know each other in ways that would never have happened in their previous everybody-running-in-their-own-direction lifestyle.

When you have finally unearthed what you love from that musty closet of time and old fears, yes, it may seem a little wrinkled and faded – but if you shake it out and put it on, the wrinkles of suppression will fall out in the fresh-air warmth of your willingness and enthusiasm, and it will start to shine its magnificent true colors through the sparkle of your joy and new aliveness. What you love, as you allow its presence to give your heart voice in your life, will lead you into a way of working which has meaning and value that is vibrant, rejuvenating and joyfully contagious. And as you continue to let love guide your purpose in whatever you do and seek, everything you create will create you anew.

When tragedy strikes: sudden love-and-purpose-changing catalysts. When tragedies occur, lives are turned upside down and everything changes. Grief plays out in as many ways and means as those experiencing it, and it is impossible to prescribe any one right way to go through it. Some who grieve may immediately take on new purpose and work that expresses a new awareness of what matters to them. To others it comes slowly over a longer period of healing, especially if the loss involves a close loved one. But it always comes if the "survivors" can survive the grief.

One massive time of collective loss and grief is when 9/11 happened. I lived in New York then, an hour north of the city, and my niece lived and went to school in downtown Manhattan. Our lives, and the lives of everyone we knew changed on that day – whether we lost our own loved ones or not. My niece happened to be on Staten Island that morning with her boyfriend. She couldn't go back to her apartment because the street where she lived had been closed off, and then they shut down Staten Island for a week or so. This, with the sudden intensity of life and awareness of its importance, led to things accelerating in their relationship, and they became engaged and later married. She also changed her work to something that allowed her to be of service to others in ways she had always loved. There were many cases of people changing their work, almost immediately. One woman I came to know whose husband had been killed started working with and supporting artists who needed patronage. A friend whose husband died in one of the planes changed her corporate job to become a counselor and fitness instructor closer to home so she could spend more time with her daughters. I remember talking with a woman who had lost her new husband of only two months, and in the middle of her grief was shocked to be experiencing the strange interloping joy of writing – something she had always wanted to do but had been afraid to try.

It is striking to realize that it was our workplaces that were targeted. Not only were personnel and physical assets of whole companies or their New York offices destroyed, but in the wake of this tragedy many people left jobs that suddenly seemed incompatible or unimportant in order to work at things that mattered to them. In thousands of ways, peoples' lives were changed that day – just as what happens with a singular or collective tragedy of any kind no matter what the cause. But in all the stories I know of personally, in every case new loves, potentials and purposes emerged from the ashes of that terrible time. And I believe that is because love and the abiding isness of life are greater inner and outer forces than any forces in the world.

Another kind of tragedy involving extended financial hardship occurred during the 2007 "Great Recession" in the U.S., when so many people lost their work and their homes, and lives changed radically. There are many stories of falling apart and rebuilding from this time, but one I remember in particular because it illustrated the opportunity for repurposing in the middle of loss. It was a news interview with a man who had lost his job, like so many others. He had never really liked his job, but he needed to work so he kept trying to get another one similar to it because of the skills he had acquired. But to no avail. He then thought "well, if I can't get paid doing what I don't want to do, I may as well work for free at something I like!" So he decided at that point he had nothing to lose by doing something he had loved since he was a kid – collecting and fixing old clocks. So he started doing that, and then began selling them online, and ultimately opened his own storefront. He said he was happier than he had been in years because doing something he loved gave him "a real sense of purpose."

There were lots of stories floating around like that during those years. What I saw happening was that as our powers of acquisition and consumption were curbed, we began to have more appreciation for what we already had, and why it mattered to us. In all circumstances and events of loss, if we look beyond our attachment to status quo and the possessions and forms we've created and become used to, it is then that we may discover the treasure trove within us of new talents and opportunities that emerge by re-purposing what we love.

Growing the seeds of love and purpose. What if you're just starting out in life and trying to get through school, make friends and have some fun times – or just survive the minefields of your surroundings – metaphorically or literally? What if you have to figure out what kind of work to do or what college or major to take up before you even have a clue who you are and what you love – especially while at the same time trying to fit in and not be so different from everybody else? Or you love to do a lot of things but you don't know how to put them together into an education or career focus.

While how it plays out often has a lot to do with exposures and opportunities that each child has, I've seen kids who had very little of those in a positive sense and yet connected with one thing they loved which not only "saved" them from the emotional and mental toll of adverse circumstances, but also purposed their lives. On the other hand, sometimes those with a lot of opportunity and interests have a harder time deciding what to pick. I've seen different degrees of lack and plenty through the young people in my life, both close loved ones and kids who worked with me on projects throughout some of their most difficult teen years.

One girl, I will call her Tara, started to package cards for me when she was about 12, and she worked with me off and on until she was 18. Her family life was terrible in so many different ways. She was always trying to protect her younger siblings, and she herself was the victim of a crime. She had little self-esteem and faith in herself, and through our years together I tried to help her with that. Just when it seemed she might entertain the notion of community college, she dropped out of high school. I encouraged her to get her GED, and she finally did. I saw a lot of potential in her and kept encouraging her about college. There was a glimmer of hope in her about it, but not enough faith she could do it.

About that time I brought my niece, Hannah, up to New York to live and work with me for the summer before she started school in the city. Hannah was very loving and beautiful, and always loved to make people feel good about themselves – and she was also, strangely, very "street" for a small-town Kentucky girl. I had her and Tara work together and saw how well they connected. So I enlisted Hannah's help to encourage Tara to go to college, but in a subtle way, over the course of the summer. Somehow that was what was needed. Peer encouragement from somebody Tara could relate to, but who had dreams, helped her to make some dreams of her own. That next semester Tara started college, and a few years later she had graduated from a four-year criminal justice school with special FBI training. It's not hard to see the thread of Tara the protector and one-time victim in Tara the FBI agent! The next thing I knew she was working in Manhattan, and I got an invitation to her wedding.

In the case of my versatile goddaughter Lindy (you may remember her from Volume 2), she grew up surrounded by good education, opportunity, and in her case, exposure to lots of writers – songwriters, poets, authors, story-tellers, playwrights and more. One day at the age of 7, she announced that she wanted to make up poems too, and she came back 10 minutes later with her own first poem that was truly amazing in wordsmithing and wisdom about the unity of the world, and a drawing to go with it! Soon we were creating her own card line, and by her tween and teen years she had become an accomplished singer-songwriter, poet and artist – and she also loved certain sciences. As she made her studious way through high school, her big brain and heart gave her a bigger-picture perspective of life that was apparent in her uncanny perceptions and wisdom. However, as the time came to look at colleges, she became very stressed about how to make sense of all her different interests and talents. One night we sat talking in the car after a movie, and she said, clearly in distress, "How do I decide so soon on a college and a major if I don't know yet what I want to be or do?"

I wanted more than anything in that moment to say something that would ease this for her. She may not remember now what I said that night, but I do because I needed to hear it myself. I told her that she didn't have to decide about forever right now, or *ever* for that matter. She only had to decide based on what she knew about herself in that moment and trust that would lead her to the next moment and the person she would be then. I told her that life will always keep presenting you with decisions, and whatever you decide, *if you allow your heart to change your mind* to go down a different road when you're called to it – then because of your heart, you will know that it is a true road at that moment – and because it is true it will lead you to the next true thing.

She is currently a sophomore in college having written much of her soon to be first novel and working on a double major in English and Geology. Her new interest in geology came through an internship working with a team on a series of television documentaries about global climate change. That work helped to expand her consciousness to the greater world and the Earth itself, and that, coupled with having "accidentally" chosen a college with a remarkable geology museum on campus, sparked her interest in something entirely new and unexpected. And so while she's still exploring and allowing her education, exposures and experiences to accumulate, she is starting to see how the different things she loves might ultimately come together as one or more multi-level career paths over the course of her life – especially the more she understands the meaning, the "why" that each of the things she loves holds for her. *Postscript*: As I was editing this paragraph, a post of hers popped up on Facebook quoting Mark Twain: "The two most important days in your life are the day you were born, and the day you find out why."

An example of cultivating purpose from seemingly no particular interests to "multiple loves" is Lindy's younger sister Sara, who, some years ago after hearing yet more praise about Lindy one day, whined in her endearing way, "what is my talent? I don't have any talents." At that point in her young life (I think about 8 or 9), Sara's talent was her quirky, vibrant, clever, *different* personality, and so we told her that. She yelled back, "that's not a talent, that's just who I am!" So she started exploring things she might have a talent for, which included bricklaying, pizza-pie making and a number of other funny kid things (she actually asked for bricks and cement one Christmas!). Then she got to the age where she started acting in school plays – always in the interesting quirky roles. And then finally, because the whole family played musical instruments, she decided she wanted to play one too, but it had to be something nobody around her was playing because she "wanted to be different."

So first it was the electric guitar (everybody else played acoustic). Then she tried the accordion. Nope, not that. Then the mandolin, but she put that down when the rest of her family picked it up. Then she took up classical guitar since they were all playing and writing pop and folk. Then, as she was exploring a growing interest in world music, she discovered the sitar and began to study seriously with a teacher almost 2 hours away. Then she saw the movie "Midnight in Paris" and fell in love with the gypsy jazz guitar, and that became her new thing. She began to write her own gypsy jazz compositions and was asked to open a show featuring a famous singer-songwriter as the headliner in a regional concert. As her skill and confidence grew, just before her 16th birthday she played in a gypsy jazz festival jam outside of Paris – and was a crowd favorite as the only young girl player. Now she is beginning to incorporate aspects of sitar "ragas" into her gypsy jazz compositions. Sara is still a young purpose-in-progress, but she's starting to see music school and more stage-lights on her horizon. Her story so far illustrates the cultivating of love, talent and purpose from seemingly nowhere, according to her – but for sure she's going somewhere!

And I want to add something else that Sara said: "Don't forget," she texted, "you also find the people you want to be around through what you love to do – I can't tell you how many people I now love that I've met through my musical adventures!" Yaayyy Sara for "grokking" this so early in your life! This is one of the wonderful ways that our love for what we do increases the love in all other aspects of our lives – through our connections and collaborations with people who are also doing what they love! This adds a whole other level to our lives and creations. During my many years of co-writing songs, any time we were all working together in a spirit of love and joy our work was compounded by an "invisible presence" of inspiration that helped us to write the song! And that would also carry over into the arranging and recording when new people came in to contribute their talents. This happens in every field of endeavor, not just the obvious creative fields. In coming together with others who have a similar love and purpose, the quantum possibilities of "where two or more are gathered, there shall I be" take full effect in creating something that is truly "greater than the sum of the parts."

So now, moving along...let's say you know what you love – at any age – and you need some practical spin on how to get your love purposed into your work. The Angel wisdoms suggest to go about it in two ways: **work your purpose**, or **purpose your work**. (Or some of both.)

Working Your Purpose

Working your purpose is when you choose work directly based on what you love and want to do – like when you know that you love music and introducing others to the joys of music, so you decide to purpose that love by getting or creating work as a music teacher. Or, as a childhood Lego-lover, you grow up and still want to build things, so you get a job as a construction worker or a contractor, or you get the education to become an architect, designer or engineer, and in the meantime perhaps you do internships to help you discover where your specific interests and strengths lie. And then ultimately you go get that job. This is working your purpose – a kind of "as the crow flies" modality – more linear and obvious, often with a lot less angst about what kind of work you're going to do because you are clear about what you love and choose your work from there. If this is you, your concerns will likely be more about *where* to work.

The thing that's important to remember as you develop a career is that jobs can come and go, but the love that gives you purpose belongs to you and will always be with you, even while that love may be growing, changing and taking on new dimensions as you do. So if you lose a job or get laid off, you haven't lost your purpose. Just where you're going to be doing it. And so – have love and purpose, will travel. You find another job doing your purpose, and if you have to do some seemingly unrelated jobs for awhile, you can use them as opportunities to develop relevant new skills, stepping stones and colleagues.

Say you are someone who loves working with kids – you love to inspire their imaginations and help them learn all kinds of new things about themselves, each other and their world. So you've done the hard part – you've figured out what you love. The second part is being willing to make that love your purpose. Once you've got those two down, there's a world of options for bringing your love and purpose to a work-place. If you have or plan to get teaching credentials, you could teach school. If not, you can pursue other ways to do your purpose – like creating innovative online programs for home-schoolers, after school tutoring, writing motivational children's books, going into schools to present special programs, and so on.

A friend of mine who is a singer-songwriter loves making music and working with kids. She used to teach music to little kids in various venues – gyms, studios, homes, parties, etc., as well as direct school talent shows and concerts. After a few years of that she got the idea to start her own day care/pre-school specializing in art, music and language programs. Currently in her fourth year with two art and language teachers assisting, she is booked to capacity, while still involved with school programs and playing in her own band – and loving it all! Her multiple loves – creating and playing music and inspiring and working with kids – compose the different aspects of her purpose, and her purpose has inspired her to continue to create new kinds of work that love her back with joy, success and the creative energy to keep doing it!

A couple other friends who love helping people to improve their lives have chosen very different career paths to express the same purpose. One is a personal trainer, and the other a motivational coach. Another who is fascinated by the workings of the human psyche is a therapist, while another is a scientist who researches the effects of biochemistry on how we feel and behave. Several people I know who love to help people who are ill to get better and resume their lives do their loves in very different ways. One is a doctor who focuses on pain and symptom management, another on well-being and preventative medicine, another is an energy healer, and another is a physical therapist.

Once you know the motivating "why" of what you love to do, which is the ballast of your ship in the sea of life purpose, then you can take your ship into any waters that express the "what" and "where" of your why – and also include other aspects that reflect who you are – like working on your own or with others, in a public or private sector, in a climate that is warm year-round or has all four seasons, or doing your thing in the country, the suburbs, the city or an island somewhere.

Purposing Your Work

Purposing your work is about bringing to the job you have aspects of what you love and enjoy. Like when your preferred job as a music teacher is not yet available, but in the English classes you're assigned to teach you show your students how to use metaphor, meter and rhyme to turn poetry into lyrics (which will get them a whole lot more interested in poetry too!). I know a teacher-musician who turned half his English classes into school choirs and bands! Or say you love interior design, but don't have an industry degree just yet, or don't plan to, but you use your job at Home Depot to help people choose their new kitchens or paint colors, or maybe you decorate your friends' houses or work as a design consultant in a furniture store. Or your job title is CEO, but what you really love to do is to motivate people – which is what makes you so good at cultivating the talent that brings success to your company. And that talent is what may lead you later into a job as a motivational speaker, a business coach or the director of a local afterschool program.

This is a way of working that is more layered and cross-pollinating – sort of a "love the one you're with" approach! Seeing the opportunity in the seeming obstacle can help you turn a "meanwhile" job into a place where you can practice and purpose your love in a different setting, or cultivate certain skills you will need for your purpose down the road.

When I think back to some of the jobs I did to support myself while I was learning to be a professional writer, I realize now that as tedious and uninteresting as some of them were, with all of them I ultimately managed to inject or extract aspects that helped to cultivate what I loved. Waitressing gave me exposure to a lot of people's life-stories-in-a-nutshell. In every case, those who loved what they did and had a sense of purpose shined with enthusiasm and generosity. Those who didn't often seemed tense and unfriendly until we got into some "real" conversation, when their pain of an unfulfilled life emerged. Their stories helped me to cultivate compassion and see the sameness in our deepest desires to be who we truly are and do something that makes us feel alive and worthwhile. I came to feel that there was nothing in the world more beautiful than the light of wholeheartedness shining in a person's face, and the seeds of my desire to inspire others to do what they loved kept growing within me.

The night-shift word-processing work I did in law firms gave me similar experiences, and also helped with some practical support of my own purposes. Those jobs not only paid my rent but also studio expenses in my early songwriting days – and it got my computer skills and typing speed up to

145 words a minute so that when I was writing I could capture the rapid-fire words that would go through my mind before they were gone. And then there were the young associates and paralegals who were being overworked into the night on a regular basis who would talk about what they *really* wanted to do, but were too afraid to abandon the expectations of family, prestige, financial goals, etc. Except for one guy who was not only brain-smart, but heart-wise. As hard as he worked you could feel that the work didn't own him, and it seemed something else was in store for him. He and his wife eventually adopted a child, and he was so inspired by the experience that he left the firm and opened his own adoption agency, using his law degree and experience to support work he loved and believed in.

As he exampled, our education and skills don't have to be used for the usual kinds of work they imply. Combine them with a passion for something we love, and there's our launch pad for finding or creating meaningful work!

Often our work grows our purpose through new exposures and influences, as the thing we love cross-pollinates other areas and yields unexpected talents within us. Like my friend Stacie Florer, who refers to herself in her new website as a "metaphysical metalsmith." A maker of unique and intricate jewelry pieces using various metals which she combines with other media, her work was seeded as a kid making shapes out of scraps of telephone wire. She wasn't thinking then she would be a jewelry artist someday – she just loved making shapes out of wires and giving them as gifts. As she grew up and had numerous adventures in her worldwide travels, the various roads in her life began to lead more and more to a crossroads. In her own words,

"I walked into a jeweler's shop in Springfield, Oregon on my lunch hour during a particularly awful day at work in a job that had become unfulfilling. The jewelry designer was at his bench, and I struck up a conversation with him. I asked him how he got started making jewelry, and he replied, 'I just started, and kept doing it every day.' I asked if one needed to go to school, and he said he was self-taught. This conversation planted a seed...which was watered a year or so later when I was in a therapy session in Portland, Oregon. I didn't know how to choose what I wanted to do with my life at 37, after moving and not having a job. My therapist responded with, 'Just watch what you do when you don't have to do anything else.' At that time it was making beaded jewelry, and so I decided to follow that and see where it led me. It led me back to myself, back to the girl that created things in telephone wire to give to others."

I met Stacie very serendipitously a few years later, after she had been working in metal for some time and her rekindled love was taking on new depth, coalesced in a phrase that came to her one day: "soul to substance." She realized that she wanted the shapes she made to come from meaning and communicate meaning in their form – for herself and for the person who would be wearing them. She began to think of her metalsmithing in terms of alchemy and as symbols that held personal resonance and transformation in life stories. As the "why" of her work has grown, that same meaning and purpose which fuels her jewelry artistry is also being expressed in co-creative conversation, teaching and writing. Each thing instructs and enhances every other thing – while all her creations are at the same time re-creating her with new understandings, new dynamics in her closest relationships and in potentials she didn't even know were inside her coming to light.

Stacie is a great example of how being open to new self-discovery is what individuation is all about: cultivating the rich versatility of who we are, and allowing our different inner and outer parts and influences to inspire and cross-pollinate rather than become compartmentalized.

Using "interruptions" to grow and exercise your purpose. In Stephen Cope's book, *The Greatest Work of Your Life*, which I mentioned earlier, he examines the lives of visionary "purposers" we all know of, such as Jane Goodall, Henry Thoreau, Beethoven and more, as well as some of Cope's own colleagues and friends who have been called to extraordinary purpose, even through difficulty and illness.

One story was about Marion Woodman, world-recognized Jungian analyst, author and teacher, who in the middle of a brilliant purposeful career was stricken with cancer and told she would die a painful death. The details of her story are remarkable, but in short, she made a conscious decision to embrace her illness – not her death – as her teacher and new "destiny" or "dharma," and she stripped her life of everything that did not support that purpose. Finally, after much suffering, which she also embraced rather than resisted, "'I persevered,' she said...in trying to experience its many shocks as symptoms attempting to bring healing—wholeness into my body-soul connection.'" (p. 166) In accepting "all of life," she accepted the fact of her illness in that *present* moment of her life, but *not* the potential *future* outcome that had been prescribed for her. **Essentially her purpose became to *love* her being into wholeness, and so she supported the wholeness rather than fighting the illness**. This enabled her to attune to what her body needed in order to be healed, so that she could exercise her choice to live.

While writing this section, I took a break to run an errand, and an inspirational short on Oprah Radio was featuring author and documentarian Kris Carr. About ten years ago at the peak of a fast-track career as an actress and photographer, she was diagnosed suddenly with a rare slow-growing stage IV inoperable and incurable cancer and was told she would likely have only about ten years more to live. She decided, after the initial devastating news, that she would reject that prognosis and embrace the "what is" rather than the *what if.* She would love all aspects of her life, including all 24 tumors, and "get busy living" wholly and fully. I later checked her out online and learned more. Instead of viewing her cancer "as a freight train to death" she began to view it "as a catalyst for change." In embracing and going toward wholeness and treating herself as a whole person, she made diet and lifestyle changes that supported her whole health and sought out doctors who would work with her on that basis. In the meantime, she purposed her new passion into a documentary and several books. She recently had her 10th year check-up, and was ecstatic to find out that her tumors were shrinking.

There are many inspiring aspects of these stories, but what is so striking to me is that neither woman regarded her illness as something she had to get out of the way so she could get back to her "real life" or "true purpose." In embracing everything in her life and body as part of the whole of herself within the whole of her life, each treated her illness as a way to seek new meaning and expand her purpose. In effect, each used her illness as an "alchemical agent" to achieve wholeness.

Most of us regard seemingly negative, or even merely unexpected, events and encounters as interruptions of our work and purpose, because we are holding a prescribed idea of how it should all play out. Imagine if we could perceive everything which happens in our lives, planned or unplanned, as an opportunity to exercise and advance our purpose, then we would look for the crosshairs of love and meaning behind whatever shows up to illuminate the "why" or "how" of our "what" in that moment. You may be trying to get a particular task finished so that you can exercise your purpose to spend some quality time with a loved one or a friend. So your purpose then is to extend love and companionship. But perhaps that person, or another, interrupts you before you've finished your task because they really need to talk to you in that moment. This is when you must remember that although you may think finishing the task will advance your purpose, the task itself is not actually your purpose. Your purpose is to love, and it's calling to you right now.

I have had many "distractions" while writing this particular volume. Urgent travel and supervising the care and affairs of an elder friend from near and far, as well as dealing with various business responsibilities and day-to-day demands of all kinds that couldn't wait – all while trying to focus on the most intense writing project I've ever undertaken – has been an enormous challenge. And the nature of this project is that it must be done in a state of utter presence and love. So either I've had to yo-yo in and out of love and presence between writing and other demands and distractions, or I've had to embrace all of it as different threads of the whole tapestry of my life and stay in love and presence with whatever part of the picture was taking precedent in any moment. Sometimes I've succeeded, and sometimes not – which meant I had to practice *returning* to love and the present moment again and again.

And this seems to be what we are called to over and over – a returning to love and the here and now from our prodigal journeys into the past or the future, worries and doubts, what was and what if. We are in a continual exchange between the inner and the outer, and riding the natural tides of ebb and flow that take things and people away and bring in the new. In the tides of our lives, love is fluid and the waters of our truths must flow toward the shores of our outer physical being and doing to gather our experiences, and then ebb back in to make sense and meaning of it all. And that is as it should be. For as the Angel wisdoms tell us again and again, life is not about arriving, but journeying – and it is not so much the miles and mountains we conquer in the outer world, but the distance we are willing to go within.

The willingness to make this journey to the Divine center of our earthly being must be renewed continually. For it is in the inner atmosphere of self-love, acceptance and compassion that the roots of Divine Love and Truth within us and in our connections with all of life are nurtured and deepened. Thus when we give ourselves to the whole – as true individuation aspires to – we, and all others, are not diminished but increased. In approaching the potential magnitude of who we are in our innermost being, we come to know that in co-creation with our inner Divine, not even the sky is a limit to what we might become!

And there is this: when we are engaged with cultivating and expressing who we truly and fully are in our commingled Divine-Human beingness, we are fully supported by the nature of Life itself – and thus Divinely assisted in ways that are most personal and relevant to each of us. But for this support to have full impact, we must "get over" our tendency to self-judgment and feelings of unworthiness. For truly, by the Divine that dwells within our humanity, we are meant "to have the moon on a string" while we are "stationed" on Earth.

If what we love is at the heart of all our being and doing, then we will attract and grow love in so many different ways in our life that we will experience living not as a spending of time, but a gathering of it. We will master the secrets of time that can reveal to us the mysteries of the eternal while we are still here. And we will leave this world richer than we came because we will have increased the only thing we can leave behind and still take with us.

Daily Life with the 72 Angels

As the year progresses and I continue in the receiving and co-creating of these daily wisdoms, and I hear about the experiences of others working with them, I am quietly amazed at the power of daily communion with the Angels in their heart dominion. Working with the wisdoms is like a daily touchstone – a "pre-set button" as one person put it – to help bring us into the moment, to the now-here where our lives are really lived – the now that is the portal to all our "hidden powers" to conjure the miraculous in the seemingly mundane – the now that enables us to access the more of who we are and long to be, so that we might bring something of great value to the world *every day*, our own loving and true selves.

Yesterday is but a husk of harvested vibrancy, and tomorrow still a seed in the winds of today, says the wisdom of the first Angel VEHUIAH. The continual challenge and opportunity to keep coming back to today, where everything in our life happens, has helped me to understand more and more that the process of becoming who we truly and fully are is not meant to be an arrival, but an ongoing journey of return to self, love and presence. And although our falterings and stumblings along the way may seem like human "foibles," these are actually the ways we are deepened and heightened while we are moving forward.

Everything we struggle with is an opportunity to peel away what lies between the world and who we truly are. And it is heart-and-mind expanding to realize that through the living of our lives, we enable the Divine within us to experience what cannot be experienced without us – and how

41

much better this life can be for us when we let our inner Divine tag along as our most intimate, co-creative, day–to-day life partner(s)!

Ongoing Work and Play with the Angels

The 72 Angels' daily wisdoms are given unto us to help increase awareness and utilization of our magnificent inner resources – the soul-voice within our hearts and our Angelic support system designed to amplify the Divine within all the inner and outer parts of our human beingness. Thus we might become the true and full Divine-Human beings we are here to be. As we begin to experience the Angels in this light, we see ourselves, each other and all of life in a light of greater potential. There is so much more to see than we are looking at, so much more to feel than we are reaching for, so much more to know than what has been handed down to us by others.

As we allow the Angels to take up more of our inner room, there is less space for doubts, fears, guilt, shame and old hurts, and more room for the truth of who we are and the self-love that enables us to truly love others. Looking through our "Angel-eyes," we see their messages and gifts waiting in the wings of every moment, encounter, conversation and coincidence. Our daily lives become full of signs, wonders, symbols and clues to unlock the meanings and purposes of our gifts, opportunities and challenges.

Through the Angels we come to understand that we each exist as a uniqueness of being and possibility within the Divine Oneness, and the Divine Oneness exists within us in order to experience life as only each of us can live it. Thus, when we welcome the Angels as *angles*, or qualities, of Divine Light – we are not asking them to come to us from "Above."

What we are actually doing is inviting our awareness to see that they are already here within and around and among us. By welcoming them, we acknowledge their presence and our willingness to engage their Divine magnificence shimmering within us as the potential of our own magnificence.

And so, as in the Divine-Human mysteries of many spiritual paths, we are called to three things in our work and play with the Angels: **ask**, **receive** and **become**. This ongoing 3-step "Angel-alchemy" can ultimately transform our base *mettle* into the spiritual gold of a being who is fulfilled in the wholeness and co-creation of love and truth:

1. **Ask** (Invoke) – Pray/chant/speak the Angel's name, open your heart and invite its presence to expand within you.

2. **Receive** (Imbibe) – Breathe in, listen, meditate upon and allow the Angel's essence and energy to expand within your heart and being.

3. **Become** (Embody) – Absorb, digest and assimilate the Angel's qualities into the very belly of your beingness so that your awareness and your action come into harmony (as in 'walking the talk').

These steps can be part of a meditation with the day's Angel and used to focus attention and awareness for everything you encounter during your day. Most importantly, follow the inner prompts from that not so still, not so small voice in your heart, for it may be the voice of the Angel within, in unison with and amplification of your own soul and its purposes. Slowly, even epiphanously, the effects become cumulative and life-transforming.

As soon as you open yourself to the Angels, they begin to work within you and things start to wake up and happen in your life naturally as rocks are rolled away from the cavern of your heart. Although grace is probably most often referenced to Christianity and the "Christ" that is the embodiment and expression of Love, grace precedes and is not exclusive to any religion, nor can anyone prescribe how it will work with you. Your grace-path is deeply personal and of utmost relevance to you and every iota of longing and circumstance in your life and being. But perhaps there is this one common aspect, as the Angel ALADIAH says, *"Grace does not happen yesterday or tomorrow – it is a present that is given only in the present, in a moment of Presence."* Whatever name or affiliation grace may ever go by, it is about the energy of a commingled Love and Truth which meets you in your heart, in whatever path, creed (or not), culture, vocabulary or circumstance. When grace happens with the Angels, you embark upon a co-creative journey that enables you to become as much or more fully and wholly human as you have ever dared to imagine.

So, my suggestion is to make some quiet time for a few moments every day to read and contemplate the day's Angel-wisdom. Remember that the message is meant to speak to your heart, and note the parts that resonate with you. As you go through your day notice what is echoed in conversations and encounters, and where you can use the qualities of that day's Angel to approach yourself and others more heartfully. Pay attention to the moments that trigger a feeling, which will indicate a timely relevance to you. Begin to see the connections between you and everything and everyone which are sometimes signaled by coincidence and unexpected encounters. And with every question you have, whatever truth you seek, consider that the answer is love – and look to what that means and what you are called to in that moment.

The Seasons of Our Lives

Despite various spiritual allusions and concepts to the contrary, the Angels tell us that this plane of existence is NOT an illusion. It is a context, an experience, a way of being that allows every aspect of God to be manifest with a life and beingness of its own – at the same time, paradoxically, as part of the totality – like leaves on one great family tree of creation. What is an illusion is to think that this world's reality, or our own outer beingness, is *all* there is. Sometimes a leaf is so far out on a branch that it has forgotten the trunk that supports it, the roots that sustain it, and the heart-sap that nourishes it. It's just out there waving in the wind, soaking in the light, shining with all its changing colors through the seasons of its life. Nevertheless for all its own forgetting, it is not forgotten by the tree itself as it continues to be sustained for all its days. And then the day comes when its form falls to the ground to become nutrients for the soil that birthed it. No longer contained and constricted in form, its essence is freed to experience that, however magnificent it was to be a leaf, it is now, and once again, far more than it was as a leaf-form. For its greater life – its essential life – is eternal.

We can learn so much from nature about being both form and essence. Thus, the Angels' daily wisdoms follow the flow and energies of the seasons expressed in the natural world and also in our own lives. Just as with the Divine and the entire cosmos since the first "moments" of Emanation and differentiation of the One into the many of Creation, everything and everyone is birthed, lives and moves forward not only seasonally, but daily, through cycles of ebb and flow in the context of **relationship**. Thus, in the first cycle of 72 messages starting March 21, there is a focus on our relationship with the Divine and our soul's cosmic birth, from which all else emerges. The 72 Angels in their daily heart dominion cycle five times a year (72 x 5 + some overlapping days = 365):

Spring ~ 3/21–6/2: <u>Relationship with the Divine.</u> The newborn green of Spring symbolizes our cosmic birth and what the soul regards as our primary relationship with the Divine Itself as our origin. Just as with the Spring rebirth of many forms of Creation in the natural world, we too experience the quickening and joy of new being as we begin to sprout new beginnings and creations that have been gestating within us during the Winter.

Summer ~ 6/3–8/16: <u>Relationship with self.</u> This is a time of exploration and celebration of ourselves through self-love, compassion, forgiveness, gladness, a lighterness of being and the flowering and ripening of our unique potentials.

Fall ~ 8/17–10/29: <u>Relationship with work and purpose.</u> This is the season for harvesting the fruits of our summer and scattering new seeds as we get back to work after vacations and times of fun and relaxation with family and friends. While outer forms begin to fall away, we begin a deeper exploration into meaning and purpose as we continue to cultivate our individuation through new ideas and projects.

Late Fall-Early Winter ~ 10/30–1/8: <u>Relationships with others.</u> Here the Angels bring us to heart-and-mindfulness about how we relate personally with others – and our reflective and sacred self that we meet within the other in casual encounters, close relationships and colleagues. In remembering and attending to what matters most with partners, family and friends, where the need for healing is often most apparent, we see the opportunity through the harvest of our own self-transformation to transform our relationships.

Winter ~ 1/9–3/20: <u>Relationship with community and the world.</u> The Angel wisdoms focus here on how we contribute the unique qualities of our individuation, purposes and interpersonal relatings to mass consciousness, even as we continue to become more and more who we are through contemplation, reassessment and the gestation of new ideas, new wisdoms and new beginnings for a refreshed, even reborn, self in the Spring.

Again, as mentioned in Volume 1, the seasonal references in the Angel wisdoms would be reversed for those in the southern hemisphere, and are perhaps less correspondent for those who live closer to the equator with less dramatic differences in the seasons.

Harvesting the Fruits and New Seeds of Fall

If you live in a four-season climate, Summer's twilight leading into Fall may be the most dramatic time of year as it goes from the harvest of nature's colorful bounty into the fiery reds, oranges and golds that, beautiful as they are, offer the last blazing spectacularity of dying forms. The sun is shortening our days quickly now as tans fade and sun-drenched revelries are exchanged for sweaters and smells of woodsmoke and nature's musky waning. Everything is telling us it's time to go back to work! Children start school, and we adults get busy with new ideas and projects and a sense of what we'd like to accomplish before the year-end holidays start up. It's a crispy, cozy time of year with crackles of change in the air – and as the Angel wisdoms sometimes say, the creation energies of love *love* change! It is from the changes of Fall that new seeds are scattered which will yield newborn beauties in the coming year.

Even more than the start of the calendar year, this is a time when we think of our work in a new way, with perspectives and purposes freshened from vacations, slower work paces and time to think. Some of us are starting new businesses or jobs, and some of us are reevaluating or reinvigorating old jobs with new ways of doing business. It's what we seed during this particular cusp of change that will carry us all the way into next Spring's new yields of growth and expansion. And so the Angels within invite us to think about what purposes we are seeding in our work, and if they sprout a true and healthy growth of who we are and what we love. For in this sowing of the next cycle of reaping, if we want our life to 'come up roses' – then we must plant rose seeds!

The Daily Wisdoms
The 72 Angels' Days of Heart Influence

In case you did not start the *Book of Days* series with the first two volumes, repeated here, with a few revisions and additions, are the various associations accompanying the daily Angel wisdoms which relate to its position on the Tree of Life, and also give clues to its nature: the Sephira and pillar of the Tree in which the Angel resides, its overlighting Archangel, astrological and date correspondences and more.

Introductory Pages: These introduce the Sephira (vessel or sphere) in which each group (choir) of eight Angels reside on the Tree of Life, as well as the qualities and functions of the overlighting Archangel.

Date: The current day of the Angel's expression through our heart plane is bolded; the other dates represent its four other "heart-days" of support during the year. Since it is helpful to be aware of your Heart Angel not only on your birthday, but also its other four days of influence, you may want to note your personal calendar with all five days. Note also that the yearly cycle for the 72 Angels begins March 21, the time of the Spring Equinox, which is the beginning of "Nissan," the first month of the year in the Jewish calendar. In my research I also ran across an obscure variant in the date attributions of the Angelic cycles, but the one used in all the *Birth Angels* materials is the cycle that the 12th-15th century school of Isaac the Blind and his followers were working with and which is most used throughout the centuries.

An Angel's full day of influence goes from 12:00 am midnight to 12:00 am midnight, 24 hours later. A few of the Angels' days overlap to support a total of 365 days. In a leap year of 366 days, the Angel for February 28 also governs the 29th. The Angels that govern for a day and a half, for example, 4/16 + 17 am, would span from 12:00 am midnight on the 16th to 12:00 pm on the 17th (midnight to midnight to noon). The "am" designation always goes from 12:00 midnight to 12:00 noon, and the "pm" from 12:00 noon to 12:00 midnight. Of course, 12:00 is a cusp minute for both day and night.

Angel's number and name: The number for each Angel represents the order of its position on the Tree of Life and its degrees of correspondence to the Zodiacal wheel of time – and if you study astrology and numerology these may give additional insight into both the Angels and the stars. The Angel's name is a transliteration of its Hebrew name. The Kabbalah also calls the 72 Angels the 72 "Intelligences" or Names of God (the "Shem HaMephorash,'), which are each composed of a three-letter combination derived from a "decoding" of Exodus 14:19-21 in Hebrew. While vowels were originally left out of the Angels' Hebrew Names to create ambiguity in order to protect the sacred Names of God, in later centuries the "niqqud" (vowel marks) were added to help with pronunciation. Each Angel's name ends in either "IAH" or "EL," denoting that the name is a Name and Quality of God. Some Kabbalists say that IAH represents the feminine aspect and EL the masculine, representing the inherent masculine-feminine unity within the Divine which is expressed as polarities within all manifestations of life (starting with, scientists believe, a positive proton and negative electron). You will notice if you consult other sources through the ages that the spellings of the Angels' names vary greatly. This is the result of dialects and permutations in the Hebrew language and its transliterations through centuries of dispersion of the Jewish people into different cultures and sects. I have done extensive research on this, but in the end have chosen to follow most of the spellings that the works of Haziel put forth based on the 12th-15th century manuscripts found in the 1975 excavation. (See Volume 1 or Appendix II herein for details.)

Pronunciation guide: This is given to help with saying or chanting the Angel's name aloud in meditation or prayer as you invite the Angel's energies to expand within you. All the names are accented (shown in ALL CAPS) on the last syllable, IAH or EL, to emphasize that the name is a quality and representation of God. Names with more than two syllables have two accented syllables.

Angel's quality/function and G/R/S designation: This represents the Divine attribute which the Angel embodies and amplifies within you, and whether the attribute is expressed outwardly (G, for "Going out" from the Divine and down the Tree of Life toward manifestation), inwardly (R for "Returning" back up the Tree to the Divine through ascending consciousness), or in a state of equilibrium which can be expressed either outwardly or inwardly (S for Stabilized).

Descriptive phrase: This is a short by-line I have added to describe the Angel's function.

Overlighting Archangel: This is the Archangel that governs the Sephira which the Angel resides within on the Tree of Life, and whose qualities overlight or influence the functions of the Angels in that Sephira and the Angelic order (choir) that the Angels belong to. There are eight Angels in each of Nine (out of Ten) Sephirot on the Tree (8x9=72). It is perhaps worthwhile to note that throughout the world's Angelic traditions, Archangels' roles regarding Earth are often viewed as the guardians of lands, nations and societal groups; whereas the Angels are attendant to individuals because their vibrations are said to be nearer to life forms.

The Angel's sign, planet and 5-day period of "Incarnation" influence: The Angel's astrological correspondences relate to its five consecutive days of influence once a year on the Incarnation, or physical, plane, which also corresponds to 5 degrees of the Zodiac (72x5=360). If you are interested in astrology, this can help to shed additional light on the Angel's qualities. (Neptune and Uranus were added later when they were discovered.) Although the Angels in their Incarnation influence (physicality, will and life purpose) are not the focus of this work, I added these dates for ease in discovering your Incarnation Angel – which would be the one governing the five-day span that corresponds to the five-days around your birth. For example, if your birthday is March 18, your Incarnation Angel would be MUMIAH, which governs March 16-20. (See the date spread next to the sign/planet indication for the daily Angel or Appendix I)

"I AM THAT WHICH…:" Here the Angel introduces itself as a particularized aspect ("that which") of the One "I AM" which is its purpose to amplify in our human lives – thus helping us to fulfill the unique "I Am That Which" that each of us are as a particular constellation of Divine-Human qualities.

The Angel's message: As explained above, all 72 Angels cycle for one day (+/-) five times a year, effectively taking us through the seasons of the year and of our lives. Since everything and everyone exists in the context of relationship, the first cycle of 72 messages starting March 21 start with our soul relationship to the Divine, and in subsequent cycles throughout the year move into our relationship with self, our work and purposes, others in our immediate circles, and the world at large. Thus, all five cycles comprise a journey in one year through all the literal and symbolic themes and seasons of our lives.

In addition, you will likely notice that the Angels have different tones – some are lighter, some more serious, some passionate even. Also, sometimes an Angel speaks as "I" and sometimes as "we." I continue to sense that in their roles as differentiated expressions of the Divine Oneness, "I" and "we" are interchangeable for them.

Note that with this volume 3, "Amen" has been added to the end of each message. I realized I had been hearing "Amen" at the end of each wisdom from the beginning of the project and had not been fully conscious of it until working on this third volume. "Amen" is a word of power in Hebrew, a kind of cosmic "abracadabra" to activate the Divine in human life. In researching the word's origins, there were the usual Hebrew and Christian uses of Amen as "so be it" at the end of prayers, as well as other correspondences: Amen encompasses the Hebrew letters "aleph-mem-nun" (confirmed, reliable, have faith, believe), which also corresponds to the word "emuna" (faith) and "emet" (truth). There are also presumed associations with the Egyptian god Amun (also Amen, the creator of all things, king of the gods) and the Hindu Sanskrit word Aum (or Om, the Absolute, Omnipresent, Manifest and Unmanifest). In suddenly becoming fully aware of the "Amen" that was naturally emerging at the end of each wisdom, I realized that the intent of the Angelic Energy was that the words would inspire and even transmit their meaning into fuller beingness within "those who have the heart to hear." In the cacophony of life and its demands, we may have the heart to hear in one moment and not in another – so the word Amen is a word to call us back to our hearts from wherever else we are. Here, it also extends a loving and compassionate space to do that, hence the three dots after the Amen…

Remember, again, that the daily wisdoms are given as messages from the 72 Angels when they are in their "heart dominion," amplifying qualities of Divine Love to support our cultivation of self-love and love of others, intuition, soul-truth and wisdom. As the Angel JELIEL conveys in Volume 1, *"the Love we bring is a Love composed of as many different qualities, forms, faces and expressions as there are people…a Love that contains all purposes and possibilities…a Love that will be your anchor against time's fickle winds of change and the sometimes stormy seas of life. A Love-light of Truth by which you may see finally that however long or far you seek, what you are looking for is always right here in your heart of hearts, prompting you to ask, beckoning you to receive, inviting you to shine forth more and more of who you truly are. And to know once and for all that, truly, you are not alone – for there is always someone at home…within."*

And so now, may you continue your daily heart-journey with the 72 Angels and the joy of harvesting the season's bounty and the planting of new seeds in your heart, mind, body and soul!

August 17 – 25

Angels 1 – 8

Sephira 1

KETHER ~ Crown/Will

Overlighting Archangel

METATRON ~ "Angel of the Presence"
Enlightenment, the connection of Light between
God's energy and human spiritual energy
(Related to the prophet Enoch & Akashic Records)

---

1 VEHUIAH

2 JELIEL

3 SITAEL

4 ELEMIAH

5 MAHASIAH

6 LELAHEL

7 ACHAIAH

8 CAHETEL

1 VEHUIAH

(vay-HOO-ee-YAH)
Will and New Beginnings (G)
'One who begins again and again'
Archangel ~ METATRON
Aries / Uranus (3/21-25)

I AM THAT WHICH...

helps you to cultivate the willingness to let your places and ways of working end and begin again as needed for your true purposes to unfold and evolve. Yesterday is but a husk of used vibrancy, and tomorrow still a seed in the winds of today. Change, which is composed of an ending and a new beginning, is used by your soul to waken your heart to a new call of love and truth that comes from within you. Though your societies often value the idea of working at the same job or in the same career for the whole of your lifetime, that is a human social value and has no particular importance at the soul level of your being. The Love that bore you forth as an expression of Itself does not care where you work or for how long at any one place – only that your work be a cultivation of your heart and soul in healthy collaboration with the rest of your parts! When you are doing work that you love using your unique talents, skills and interests, you are not only bringing more of who you are into fullness and joy of being, but you are also grounding aspects of the Divine on Earth through your own true individuation. Thereby you may also inspire others to do the same, in their own unique ways.

You are a Divine-Human being. And though you must attend compassionately to the needs of your humanity, in order to be happy and fulfilled you must also answer the call of your soul which dwells within and speaks through the feelings and truths of your heart. Be willing to allow your heart to change the set of your mind and the path of your feet. Allow new vistas to broaden the sky of your dreams. Scale your personal mountains – but when you get to the top you will realize that the high peaks can also be dead ends unless you are extending one hand toward the greater horizon that beckons and the other to those on the trail behind you who long for sky as well.

Change is often hard, especially in light of the demands and responsibilities of physical life. But in the light of love, all things are possible, all mountains are moveable, and all which desires to be given is simply waiting on your willingness to receive. When it seems you cannot muster your assertive will to make the changes that need making, then humbly allow its softer side that is **willingness** *to open your heart and mind and lead you forward.*

My light as VEHUIAH can help you to let go of the past, while also conveying all its gifts of knowledge and experience into the soil of today to help nourish the new growth emerging from within you. This 'angle' of Divine Light which I Am within you is given to remind you that even if it seems that endings are not always of your choosing, how to begin again IS certainly your choice. And if you choose with heart at your helm and the light of your inner Divine as your illuminating compass, you will always be able to find your true north – wherever the world may be pulling you. Amen...

3/22 * 6/4 * **8/18** + **19**am * 10/31 * 1/10

2 JELIEL

(YAY-lee-EL)
Love and Wisdom (G)
'One who uses love to make wisdom'
Archangel ~ METATRON
Aries / Saturn (3/26-30)

I AM THAT WHICH...

supports new beginnings and times of change and decision-making in your work-life by helping you to remember and go toward what you love in your choice of work and in the ways you work. This may ultimately involve changing the kind of work you do or where you work – but these decisions will bring new energy into not only your work, but all parts of your life if 'what' and 'where' are guided by **why** *and* **how**. *If the how and why are about love, then your work goes beyond paying the bills, taking care of family, buying things you need and want and so on. When you work with love, work becomes purpose, no matter what kind of work it is! As a Divine-Human being, your soul purpose on this Earth is to feel, know, be and do love, and it is your human right and privilege to fill in the details with your choices of where, what, when, who and how.*

For many people, work and purpose are different things, with purpose relegated to hobbies and 'outside' activities. But for some these are the same, and their lives are likely far richer than their paycheck could afford. Your world promotes the ethics of hard-work, success, responsibility, 'getting ahead' and not getting left behind. Often, however, getting ahead means leaving your heart behind. Consider that the purpose of your **vocation** is to give **voice** to your being. Your true voice comes from your heart – and as whispered and tiny as it seems inside you, when it speaks out loud it has a timbre that can be heard around the world, because it is the voice of Divine within you speaking through you, for you and as you as no other voice can.

Whether you work for someone else or at your own endeavors, work can easily become your taskmaster and a drain on your zest for life unless it is connected to your true passions – in other words, what you love. If you need a change and don't know what kind of work to do, and you continue to work at a job that is frustrating, fatiguing, depressing and unsatisfying, then you have likely forgotten what you love or that working at what you love is even an option. And it may be you forgot because you decided at some point that what you loved wouldn't love you back, wouldn't get you other things you wanted, or that it wouldn't have financially practical or lasting value in the world. Thus you put your heart's desire 'out of mind' so as not to live with the longing or pain of abandoning the truth of yourself. There is a way, however, to begin to bring back what you love by first learning to 'love the work you're with.'

No matter what kind of work you do or where, or how long or briefly you intend to do it, you can transform it into a soul purpose if you do it with whole-heartedness. This means bringing yourself to every task – as well as to your co-workers, collaborators, clients and even your seeming adversaries – with enthusiasm, willingness, creativity and integrity. For when you work with heart, the love and *enthusiasm you bring to your work is matched by the work itself through new opportunities and liaisons and increasingly higher levels of functioning, collaboration and productivity. Love is the catalyst for 'alchemy' – bring love into the mix and it transforms knowledge and experience and anything else you bring to it into wisdom. You will become the master of your work rather than the servant. Your 'have-to's' will turn into 'want-to's,' and in so doing the needs of both your soul and your work will be served at deeper and higher levels. You will become wise with the wisdom of one who chooses life rather than being decided upon. You will come to understand that the work you do is the love you do – that any work is an opportunity for love-in-action, for the gathering and exchange of creativity and knowledge, and the possibility for deeper interaction with others. From this inner bearing of dignity and self-respect, that which you truly love which has been hiding deep down inside will begin to feel that it's 'safe to come out' – that it won't be quashed, cast aside or ignored this time. And what a re-union that will be!*

Dear one, my light as JELIEL is given to help you heed the truth-voice of your heart and soul and change the what or how of your work to better serve the truth of you – rather than allowing your work to change you into someone who is not true. For the love inside you that wants to play in the world also wants to work in the world. If you let it, your work will become effortless! Amen...

3/23 * 6/5 * **8/19**pm + **20** * 11/1 * 1/11

3 SITAEL

(SIT-ah-EL)
Construction of Worlds (G)
'One who loves creations into being'
Archangel ~ METATRON
Aries / Jupiter (3/31-4/4)

I AM THAT WHICH...

helps you to create structures that bring meaning into matter, so that your matter matters! Your world is composed of the seen and the unseen, form and essence, quantity and quality, matter and meaning. The greatness of your creations is birthed in the collaboration between the inner and outer nature of things. Structure provides the opportunity for what is formless to take shape, what is unseen to be perceivable, what is unknown to become knowable and what is felt to be expressed. As architects, designers, artists, creators and builders of all things know, structure that is alive and vibrant is one that provides opportunity for flow and feeling, which supports the meaning and evolution of both the structure and its purpose. Physical life is where form and the unformed meet to create a third thing that neither can be without the other. As your body gives your soul 'legs to stand on' and lips to speak, so does the work you do provide a podium from which you may expand your presence and purpose in the world.

All manner of structures you create have the potential to create expansion or limitation. When you create structures with the foundation stones of love, truth, beauty and integrity – then the structures house the living energy of inspiration and the power to live on when structural forms fall or fade in time. It is very compelling to become enamored with the structures of your creations, but the value of what you create is in its capacity to ground and support meaning and spirit, i.e., what you truly and deeply value. This is as much true for the structures created by hand and machine as those created by feeling, thought and belief. If your creations become fixed and petrified into dogmatic and immoveable beliefs – then you are tethered to something that is structure only and has ceased to be alive or life-affirming. But if your structures remain fluid and responsive to the love and truth in their content, then they can adapt and grow with your creations.

Thus, as you give the structure of practice to your meditation or spiritual devotions or certain routines for raising children or managing the errands and busyness of daily life, allow your structures to be both solid and malleable so that they may follow the spontaneity and flow of essence. Let your structures have bending places in them – like the knees and elbows in your own limbs. Live and work with knees bent, so to speak, so that you may be responsive to the changing landscapes of life, love and truth and the winding roads they sometimes lead you down.

Thus, if you are a writer, let your table of contents be written in 'sand' rather than 'stone' during the writing of your book to allow new ideas and concepts to emerge. If you are an artist, use your drawing as a guide but allow the colors to lead your brush beyond the lines. If you are a craftsman, allow your hands to be guided by your heart. If you are a manager or a leader, allow those actually doing the work to show you a better way. If you are the builder of empires, populate your domains with ideals, creations and governors that help to bring forth more life and meaning for all – rather than implementing structures that feed off its own creators and creations into depletion and ruin.

My SITAEL light dwells within to remind you to construct your works with heart so that they will have fluidity and universality – able to meet the fluctuating needs of you as the maker, your creations and those who partake of them. Use my warming light to soften that which is rigid and unbendable, to illuminate what is hidden and longs to be expressed, to heal the fear of flow and embrace the unknown yet beautiful new life energies that flow brings. Let me be the ground that launches you skyward and gives you a place to return, the banks that give stability yet winding way to your river of life, the world that gives your heart and soul time and place to bring all that you are and desire to become into being. Blessings, dear one, upon all your creations and constructions, that they may express and expand the Divine through you and as you upon this beauty, bounty and privilege of Earth. Amen...

3/24 * 6/6 * **8/21** * 11/2 * 1/12

4 ELEMIAH

(eh-LEM-ee-YAH)
Divine Power (G)
'One who implants the tree of life within'
Archangel ~ METATRON
Aries / Mars (4/5-9)

I AM THAT WHICH...

helps to stabilize and ennoble your inner resources so that your works and creations might be imbued with true and right use of power. True power is not a force but a creation energy of love and purposeful presence. Anything that takes away your presence robs you not only of your initiative and focus, but also your access to the eternal from which your creations draw their greater power. Thus, my power is to help balance elements that become chaotic when an inner storm is brewing. My light within can help to calm torments and tempests of the mind (air) caused by conflicts among base instincts (earth), emotions (water) and desires, urges and impulses (fire). When these elements are returned to equilibrium within you, your clarity and personal power are available for your work and the cultivating of your purposes in that work.

Work and purpose are not always the same thing, though they can be two parts of the same whole. Think of work as the outer action, and purpose as the inner motivation and meaning. In addition, purpose itself operates on two levels in any work you do – the purpose of the work itself to come into fruition, and the cultivation and fruition of your own being which work can serve as a context for. Your 'being purpose' and your work purpose are each most powerful if they are in harmony and help to inspire and facilitate each other. This happens when you are doing what you love and loving what you do. Whether as vocation or avocation, compensation or speculation, the key to the vitality and success of you and your work is wholehearted purpose mixed with wholehearted effort.

All work presents you with the opportunity for learning and honing certain talents and skills, as well as the cultivation of integrity, commitment and quality that can support your purpose. You may change your work every day or year of your life – but your purpose is being defined, revealed and cultivated throughout your entire life in your every undertaking. Reflective of your reason for being, your purpose is held in your soul and thus is a living breathing aspect of your vitality.

My light within you as ELEMIAH, working through your heart, can help to empower your work and purpose with the creation energy of love and the awareness that nothing you do need be wasted or inconsequential when you see its underlying potential to empower and increase the love that you are. Thus, let us bring you as love to whatsoever you do, that you will come to recognize love as your only true power. Amen...

3/25 * 6/7 * **8/22** * 11/3 * 1/13

5 MAHASIAH

(ma-HA-see-YAH)
Rectification (G)
'One who returns to what is true for love's sake'
Archangel ~ METATRON
Aries / Sun (4/10-14)

I AM THAT WHICH...

brings to light and helps to heal disharmonies between your work and soul-purposes caused by contradictory values and actions in different aspects of your life. Rectification is always about restoring communication and collaboration between the inner and outer aspects of your being, so that you might express your life from a state of wholeness rather than as the sum of dissociated parts. There are many in your world who harbor secret personal miseries, 'sins' or offenses while doing good and great works publicly. You may tell yourself that what you do in one part of your life will not affect another part – but as time shows, this is simply not true. For in the essential unity of life, the whole is always affected by the parts, and well-being needs all your parts operating under the same value system. The disharmonies that you will not allow into your consciousness will take root in your body – or even within the psyches of family and colleagues, as well as in your own creations and endeavors. Without awareness and healing, sooner or later disease, disharmony and division will sprout from the hidden seeds of conflict, hypocrisy, distorted values, shame, guilt or other

67

contaminants. You may even secretly think or hope that your better parts will 'atone' for the lesser – but this is thinking that belongs only to your world. In the 'other-worlds' of the heavens, no one is sitting in judgment upon you. And there are no punishments beyond your world – only the natural cosmic law that life reaps whatever is sown, and that in the cradle of awakening there is always the opportunity to be nourished and restored by the light of Divine Love – both on Earth and in the heavens.

All that said, your soul is so great and so desiring to manifest its purposes within your humanity, that it will use whatever context you choose in order to do so. And though you are so loved that we wish you always utmost harmony and joy, we know that wholeness sometimes takes a long and winding road back to itself if that is what is needed for greater understanding on the journey.

So I invite you to partake of my MAHASIAH light each new day to move toward healing any discrepancies of value and vitality among your parts and restore them into your whole. By aligning your true values and purposes with both your personal and work life, they will become complementary and conducive to each other. If you show us what you love and desire to create from the wholeness of who you are, and you are willing to step out on some limbs in your heart to be in the world with that truth, then we will help you take quantum leaps, and we will lend you wings to fly. So go ahead, dear one – climb the tree of life within your heart, for in this your most sacred inner sanctuary, every limb will hold your new lightness of being. Amen...

3/26 * 6/8 * **8/23** * 11/4 * 1/14

6 LELAHEL

(LAY-la-HEL)
Light of Understanding (G)
'One who transforms knowledge'
Archangel ~ METATRON
Aries / Venus (4/15-20)

I AM THAT WHICH...

helps you to perceive and define your soul-purpose by weaving together your interests, passions and learning which, even since childhood, have been preparing you with the gifts and skills needed for the true expression of yourself. It is important to understand that your purpose may not be named by your job title or your job description – but rather **how** *and* **why** *you do your job. Ultimately, the desire of your soul, which underlies any kind of work you choose to do, is to experience the joy of individuation and the sense of meaning and worthwhileness that comes with contributing the fruits of your labors of love to others.*

For example, you may be an executive whose company designs industrial parts, and perhaps your job description has to do with product development. But through your gifts of empathy and your understanding of what motivates people to care about their work – your real purpose is about people development – encouraging and rewarding creativity and collaboration, which in turn increases innovation and productivity for the whole company. Perhaps you're a hairdresser whose customers are not only getting their hair done, but their heads and hearts tended to. Or a jewelry artist who makes one-of-a-kind pieces that help others to feel beautiful in their own one-of-a-kindness. Perhaps even a celebrity whose notoriety feels naggingly empty until it dawns on you that fame provides a podium for a greater purpose, something close to your heart that you now have the means to do.

You may struggle to understand your purpose, but it is not found 'out there' somewhere in what other people are doing – though you may be inspired and recognize bits of your purpose in other people's purposes. Or you may even be distracted from your own purpose by wanting what others have who are doing their own purpose. But as seductive, fame-inducing and lucrative as the occupations and preoccupations of others may be, the details of your own purpose can only be found in that small place inside you from which all big and far-reaching things come: your own true heart. Your purpose – your true work – is about doing what you love, with love enough to override fears, doubts, worries and seeming impossibilities. And it is only your heart – with its qualities of insight, intuition, wisdom-making and courage – that can do all that and more!

My light as LELAHEL is given to help you come to a deeper understanding of why it is important to your happiness to purpose what you love. It is because of the truth that you ARE love, and love wants always to bring more of itself into beingness. And the further truth about love is that everything love creates is one-of-a-kind. And so dear light-seeking one, the only way you can give something to the world that is truly unique is to create from the love and truth of who you are. Amen...

3/27 * 6/9 * **8/24** * 11/5 * 1/15

7 ACHAIAH

(a-KA-hee-YAH)
Patience (G)
'One who brings the stillness'
Archangel ~ METATRON
Taurus / Mercury (4/21-25)

I AM THAT WHICH...

helps you to cultivate a state of attentive receptiveness for that which is on its way to you while you work with presence, intent and integrity toward that which you desire to achieve. Patience is a willingness to be in the flow of your life and your work with a posture of faith that all things are happening at the right time for the right reasons, and that fruition will come when all variables are ripe. Worry, doubt and fear fade away and are replaced by a sense of gratitude and anticipation without hurry. This is the time, while what you desire is on its way to you, to prepare inner and outer space. It is the way a bride prepares on the morning of her wedding, or an expectant mother opens her heart as she readies cradle and home for the new one on its way. Or the small logistical steps taken or built for the launch of a dream or purpose before you even know its full magnitude. Faith and an expectant sense of flow accumulate a critical mass of your own presence as an attracting point, and preparation amplifies your resonance which attracts that which you are waiting for. There is no more compelling vibration for the fruition of your goals than that which the certain and faith-full heart transmits.

I, ACHAIAH, invite you to use the light of my patience to help you keep faith with the 'yes' in your heart even while the nay-saying of the world or your own inner detractors may be closing doors around you. It is the nature of fear and doubt and past disappointments, in all their heaviness, to quash that which you love. So just let your love be too big to flatten! No matter what the circumstances, it is always in love's power to create the impossible! If you don't entertain internal or external debunkers, they will lose interest in you – so keep trekking with your heart in full throttle headed for what you love, without assumptions or judgments. Keep going and doing and being with your sense of purpose, even while it is still evolving, and trust stillness and a seeming lack of manifestation as a time of gestation and preparation for both you and that which is on its way to you. And then, make a bowl of your heart in a desert full of those tired old doubts in readiness for the impending rain/reign of success! Love it enough to let it show up in an unexpected form. For nothing knows what you truly need more than love itself. Amen...

3/28 * 6/10 * **8/25** * 11/6 * 1/16

8 CAHETEL

(KA-heh-TEL)
Divine Blessings (G)
'One who conducts the flow of plenty'
Archangel ~ METATRON
Taurus / Moon (4/26-30)

I AM THAT WHICH...

brings a sufficient flow of light and energy for the fullness of fruition to both the inner and outer terrains of Earth and the humus of your own life and creations. As plantings come into their season of fullness, a more intense light-nourishment is given for full vitality and ripening. Because of this, what is harvested contains more life-giving nutrients and healthier seeds for future creations. In your own human endeavors, this is the time to give an extra measure of feeling and focus to 'take it all the way,' so that your success may be true and life-affirming for yourself and those who will receive the fruits. As the natural world is preparing to display its glorious colors for the harvest time, so likewise be prepared to let the fruition of your own colors shine and sparkle in the nowness and its harvest, which has surely already seeded the next thing. Celebrate with gratitude and sharing for whatever is given, for these will be your most potent 'fertilizers' for new plantings.

In all your seasons of endeavor and enterprise, we wish you to know this: there is no such condition in the universe as lack. All is plenitude – and in keeping with the universal movements of contraction and expansion – the cyclical ebbs and flows that create contrast to move all of life forward – plenitude must at times empty itself out to make room to receive the next wave of plenitude! In your life, your work and purpose, there must be times of receding in order to deepen, broaden and stimulate the creation of new opportunities. If you 'rue the day or blame the night,' you will miss the dawn's new becoming. If you resist change, you will not be ready to receive bounty from a new resource. 'If you focus on the hole at the bottom of your cup, you will miss the whole that keeps filling you back up.' There are blessings all around you, but it is the blessings within you that enable you to see and partake of them.

Thus, dear blessed one, use my light as CAHETEL to see that your greatest inner blessing is to know that you are a Divine-Human being – fully equipped to meet whatever your life serves up or 'spirits away.' Say yes to life and you will ALWAYS find the blessing that awaits your recognition. Say yes to life and you will transform every no, every seeming impossibility, into a new opportunity. Say yes to life, and life cannot help but say yes to you because you ARE the blessing of life, and life always lovingly seeks the expansion of itself. Amen...

August 26 – September 2

Angels 9 – 16

Sephira 2

CHOKMAH ~ Wisdom

Overlighting Archangel

RAZIEL ~ 'Secrets of God'
Spiritual guidance, keeper of wisdom
and revealer of the mysteries

---

9 HAZIEL

10 ALADIAH

11 LAUVIAH

12 HAHAIAH

13 YEZALEL

14 MEBAHEL

15 HARIEL

16 HAKAMIAH

9 HAZIEL

(HA-zee-EL)
Divine Mercy and Forgiveness (S)
'One who sees with the light of love'
Archangel ~ RAZIEL
Taurus / Uranus (5/1-5)

I AM THAT WHICH...

helps you to cultivate a compassionate wisdom for new beginnings in your doings and endeavors by forgiving your past so that you might carry its gifts forward into a more loving and empowered present. Dear one, we say ever so gently – accept and forgive your disappointments and hurts, for you are here to heal, not harbor, them. Be grateful for the fruit of their teachings and the new opportunities that always come with a new day. For your willingness to heal is directly proportionate to your ability to evolve and fulfill your potential in all you do. This is because your hurting parts hold the rest of you hostage to pain and unforgiveness. This not only makes those parts of you unavailable to the fullness of joy and success, but as your saying goes, 'a chain is only as strong as its weakest link.' Your harbored hurts weaken and disempower the rest of you – however brave a face, shrug of shoulder or steely determination you may show the world. Heal your karma (harbored transgressions to yourself and others) and you will be free to pursue your dharma of a meaningful and purpose-filled life of service to your Divine-Human potential and your fellow beings.

We wish for you to be unburdened by dogmatic concepts of original sin, for humanity is not inherently tainted – but inherently pure. In the vast Love and Truth of the Divine from which your essence is born, there is no judgment and thus nothing ever to forgive. There is only opportunity for exploration and learning, which happens more quickly when you are not self-judging. We also suggest that if there were to be any such thing as 'sin,' it would be judgment itself. For in the presence of judgment, all things and beings are limited, if not impossible, in their potential – and this goes against the nature and right of all life to always be growing and expanding. The true and sacred use of judgment is as an energy of temporary contraction – a pulling back which allows time and space for evaluation and course-correction, for example, a re-purposing of one's attributes and talents toward more life-affirming directions, or the revamping of a work project or business to reflect more value and meaning.

*My light as HAZIEL is **for giving you back to yourself** by dissolving self-judgment or a distorted sense of karmic punishment that life must be inflicting on you as a 'tit for tat.' You do sow what you reap – although not from a place of moral punishment, but as a natural universal law of 'like attracts like' that is not personal, yet does have a personal effect on your life. Take judgment out of your past and present, and you will quickly see the gifts of learning that can enable you to move forward more productively as you take them truly to heart. For through the heart's love and wisdom, all things, beings and endeavors are understandable and repurposeable. Go forth unyoked and lightened, dear one, for you are a cherished one-of-a-kind child-star in a universe that is waiting for your light. Amen...*

3/30 * 6/12 + 13am * **8/27** * 11/8 * 1/18

10 ALADIAH

(a-LA-dee-YAH)
Divine Grace (G)
'One who endows you with the yes of life'
Archangel ~ RAZIEL
Taurus / Saturn (5/6-10)

I AM THAT WHICH...

helps you to find your true place and purpose in your world by bringing you into your heart so that you might remember what you love and heal those things that have separated you from your love. Grace is many things to all, but always personal. It is the love that knows what you need when your need is too great to even want. It is the help that love gives to you when you feel that you cannot help yourself. It is the awareness that you are so much more than what you see in any mirror of your or another's making. It is the sudden awakening of the truth that lives within you waiting on your willingness to be so. It is the realization to your core that you are not alone, and that you are known and felt, watched over and breathed into life ongoingly from Life Itself inside and all around you. It is the dawning understanding that with your assent and enthusiasm, Life and Love and Truth work together to help you fulfill the destiny of your dreams and the purposes that you are empowered every day to bring to light. It is the miracle of transformation that rebirths you from any hurt or disappointment. It is an endless number of second chances and the ultimate understanding that there is no need to earn the love that is already yours.

In every instance of your life when you don't know what to do with yourself or your work or circumstances, it is likely because you have forgotten or put aside what you love. However intelligent you may be, you cannot answer the important things in your life through intellect alone. You must feel your way, and let the truth of your feelings take your thinking and understanding to greater heights. When you quash your feelings, you quash your power at all levels. Feelings are not fixed fact, but fluid and ever-evolving clues to the truth of you. Heeding your feelings frees them to not only express your truth, but to allow truth itself to change and evolve your purpose even as it comes to light.

So dear precious one, I, ALADIAH, invite you to come to the threshold of your heart's innermost altar and announce yourself! – 'I am here, naked and undefended, clothed only in my existence and my deep desire to be true and whole.' And dear brave one, in such a moment when you likely feel anything but brave, we shall come Godspeed from within and above and below and all around to attend you. And evermore, we shall be your reminder to live with a sense of wonder that there is always more to the meaning of your life than your five senses can reveal. And though you may be sometimes battered about in the brambled forest of the world's delights and distractions, make your way to the chapel of your heart and you will be given the grace you seek, again and again. Amen...

3/31 * 6/13pm + 14 * **8/28** * 11/9 * 1/19

11 LAUVIAH

(LO-vee-YAH)
Victory (G)
'One who turns every moment into a win'
Archangel ~ RAZIEL
Taurus / Jupiter (5/11-15)

I AM THAT WHICH...

helps to bring the realization of a dream or a sudden positive shift in circumstances through a seemingly insignificant act or effortless victory after a long time of dedication and hard work. While there may be many reasons success can seem long in coming, it is the nature and desire of the Divine within you that you and all of life shall flourish. Like a flower that was a seed in the dark soil of the Earth, you too must go through seeding times in the humus of your own being in order to receive the inner nourishment needed to create the brilliance of your blossoming. Your victories in life are not only the obvious ones that all can see. Those are just the result of the deeper victories of courage, endurance and all the inner furrowing of heart, mind and soul that goes into your ultimate magnificent expressions.

Victory for your aspirations is not a matter of deserving, but of ultimately reaping what you have sown as a basic law of nature. If you plant a flower, you get a flower. If you plant love, you will get love in one form or another. If you plant seeds of doubt, you get whatever can hesitantly push up through that, if anything. Sometimes your soul may take you the long way around to give the rest of you more time to become truly ready to receive. Or perhaps other people and situations need to evolve to be part of your success as well. Sudden victory usually indicates that finally all your inner and outer 'ducks are in a row' at the same time and place. You and all your parts are ready, your team is ready, and the world is ready for you as well.

So dear one, I, LAUVIAH, say to you – do not judge or descend into feelings of unworthiness for the time it takes to manifest the tangible results of your efforts. While you are working and actively waiting and trusting, see yourself through the magnificent light that I and all your Angelic helpmates see you – triumphant in the willingness of your heart to believe in what is not yet visible to your eyes. We bow down to you in awe of this. And so allow me to accompany you and illuminate that well-worn path of return to your heart and the love that got you started, for it will be that love that keeps you going and finally takes you the rest of the way. Amen...

4/1 * 6/15 * **8/29** * 11/10 * 1/20

12 HAHAIAH

(ha-HA-ee-YAH)
Refuge, Shelter (G)
'One who is a beacon of shelter within'
Archangel ~ RAZIEL
Taurus / Mars (5/16-20)

I AM THAT WHICH...

provides a refuge of reverie and respite from the outer world so that consciousness and clues for meaning and purpose can emerge easily from your innermost being. There is a prevailing sense in your modern societies that unless you are busy accomplishing something tangible you are wasting time. However, your power to seed new life and grow your purpose is vitally dependent on the cycles of dormancy and gestation that help to re-gather energies from deeper levels of your being. As artists and inspired creators know, it is often in the moments of not doing or striving – when you are 'taking a break,' daydreaming and 'wool-gathering' – that your greatest truths and inspirations come. The refuge of your vibrant inner domain is your most fertile 'field of dreams' from which all your doings are born. Through sleep and dreaming, daydreams, meditation and relaxation you gain access to your inner terrains and the universal resources that are not bound by time and place. From here you can go anywhere – to other ways of knowing, being and doing beyond structures, rationales and hierarchies, and to the life beyond life as you know it and the vast spirit realms from which your soul is origined. Here is your soul most at home, and here is where it is comforted, replenished, inspired and purposed from beyond all limitation.

You are a four-part being composed of soul, heart, mind and body. Each part of you needs its time of timelessness, its cessation from doing and shelter in an often stormy world of dissonant desires, responsibilities and demands. Where inside you and in the world does your soul find refuge and shelter? Where your heart, your mind, your body? Of course, what is good for one part is ultimately good for the whole and wholeness of you – as you may feel when you have a soothing massage attended by a caring healer and meditative music with no words, only the peace of stillness and being. Or perhaps there is an activity or hobby or a certain kind of non-activity you enjoy that restores your whole being. Restores, not depletes – that's the key!

I invite you to take on the mantle of my light as HAHAIAH to come home to your heart and do loving and compassionate things for yourself often – and feel how flow is restored to all aspects of your life. From your own personal cohesive and self-healing refuge, simplicity and clarity flower. What matters most becomes gently apparent and your soul purposes coalesce naturally without stress and straining. And from here, dear one, your relationship to time may be transformed so that it is no longer your taskmaster but your tool – always bringing you and your purposes back to the power and potency of the present. Amen...

4/2 * 6/16 * **8/30** * 11/11 * 1/21

13 YEZALEL

(YAY-za-LEL)
Fidelity, Loyalty and Allegiance (G)
'One who inspires faith with the inner Divine'
Archangel ~ RAZIEL
Gemini / Sun (5/21-25)

I AM THAT WHICH...

helps you to keep faith with your own inner realms and the soul truths and purposes that are broadcast to your heart, and from there to all your parts and the outer world. When you speak of being true to yourself, are you not usually referring to who you are on the inside – what you really feel and want and what means most to you? As a Divine-Human being, you will naturally be pulled between your core values and feelings and your more immediate physical, mental and emotional desires, appetites, needs and responsibilities. You are not here to suppress or exclude 'matters of the flesh' or the outer world, but rather to ennoble and expand the capacity of your human substance and your presence in the world with your inner soul-essence. The body and mind can pantomime meaning, but only the heart and soul can generate it. And yet with cohesiveness and wholeness consciousness, body and mind give time, place, movement and tangible manifestation to meaning. Thus, by using your inner being as your source from which to draw love, truth, wisdom and purpose, you will be able to put into motion nobler motivations and methods in all you do and strive for.

This kind of loyalty to your inner self will require you at times to have faith in what has not yet manifested in the physical world. This is when allegiance to your heart must be greater than to your eyes. For as your wise ones have spoken so truly, 'It is only with the heart that one can see rightly; what is essential is invisible to the eye.' To keep faith with what you know to be true from the greater knowing of your own within is one of the greatest gifts you can give to yourself – and from here will be yielded your treasure unto the world and all of life seen and unseen.

And so dear one, draw from my YEZALEL light to keep faith with yourself – especially in times when your allegiances are greatly tested. And know that loyalty to your inner being is loyalty to the Divine Self that lives within you. It is the manifestation of your own true will and purpose that is the Divine will for you. In expressing your self and your life thusly, you are thereby empowered to express a particular human image and likeness of the Divine. All other images outside of you that would draw you away from this utmost love and truth of you are hearsay and counterfeit. Be true, be you, and be the love that makes the truth of you possible in the world. Amen...

4/3 * 6/17 * **8/31** * 11/12 * 1/22

14 MEBAHEL

(MAY-ba-HEL)
Truth, Liberty and Justice (G)
'One who is freed by Truth to set Truth itself free'
Archangel ~ RAZIEL
Gemini / Venus (5/26-31)

I AM THAT WHICH...

brings the understanding that a justified life is one that is lived for the expression of your heart-truth so that you may become free to manifest your soul-purpose. The highest expression of your Divinely-endowed humanity is to experience and contribute to the world the love and truth of yourself, for in this is your uniqueness, your joy and your opportunity to offer something truly valuable to others. This is your right and your privilege, and the right and privilege of each and all beings. To your soul, it is your duty, your challenge and your greatest calling – and it can only be fulfilled on Earth with your choice and your willingness. When you exercise these, you activate the Divine and life itself to assist you. Say yes, and a way will be made. Take the first step, and a road will appear. Keep going, and you will be given guidance and shelter along the way. Follow the call of truth for the sake of love, even though the way be dark and winding, and the truth will lovingly set you free. And as you become free, you will free truth itself to evolve, expand and seek new heights – and take you with it.

While this may sound lofty, it is ultimately about creating a life that is not complex or complicated, but more simple and straightforward. That is not to say it is easy to pursue a life in which you exercise your right to be true to yourself, for the menu of options in Earth-life features a multitude of appetizing offerings, many of which are certainly worth tasting! And there is much influence among you to be like each other, to conform in ways that enable you to more easily belong and interact with your social groups and communities. But the most relevant and honorable 'road less traveled' for you and each being is the one that leads to the self, the heart, the inner treasure from which all your gifts to the world will be given. This is the road that leads to the true life that is a free life, a loving, just and righteous life.

So dear sojourner, I invite you to use my light as MEBAHEL to see that 'the one you are ever looking for is the one looking,' and that the only person ever worth being is the one no one else can be. Follow the love in your heart to discover the truth of your life, and we will be with you every light-step of your way. Amen...

4/4 * 6/18 * **9/1** * 11/13 * 1/23

15 HARIEL

(HA-ree-EL)
Purification (G)
'One who uses the light to wash clean'
Archangel ~ RAZIEL
Gemini / Mercury (6/1-5)

I AM THAT WHICH...

helps to foster integrity and right motivations in your work-life so that what you truly value is reflected in what and why you create, the way you work and how you come together with others to achieve beneficial goals. Every day you may encounter practical reasons to compromise your personal integrity and values – a 'to-do list' that needs to get done, a deadline you're expected to meet, a 'boss' or an outcome that holds the reins of your future, rent that needs to get paid or crippling debt. It is in your dual nature as a Divine-Human being to be pulled between the purity that your heart and soul seek and the needs of your physical survival and desire for success and belonging. But it is a pitfall of the 'age of specialization' to think that you can practice a different value system for one part of your life and not have it affect the other parts. 'It's just business' has become a catch-phrase for excusing impure and harmful acts, when the nobler challenge is to use your creativity to develop ways of working that are compatible with your personal values. Would you want your loved ones to partake of the fruit of your labors? Would you feed your own children the food your company manufacturers? Would you invest your own savings with the brokerage firm that employs you?

Undimmed, your purity is like a shining pearl in the heart of your being radiating the love and truth of who you are. Like sand on the sea bed, the pure light of who you are might be disturbed at times by the tides of life, but the pearl itself is still there. It is the choice and opportunity of your individuation-path to bring your purity forward to shine through how you live and work and purpose your life every day. Sometimes your personal integrity may be put in jeopardy to accommodate work agendas, and you may have to make a hard choice. Purity does not ask you to be unrelenting, inflexible or unmoving – however, the purity inside you will likely flinch at what is inauthentic or dishonest, or which serves the interests of a certain few at the expense of others. Living and working from your personal truths may unsettle those around you at times, but any truth that is carried forth by the love that you are has the potential to stimulate true and right actions of others. And yet realize even in this that your noble 'stances' must occasionally be purified, lest self-righteousness seep into them. And while purity is an often-used soapbox to cover up one's own secret shames, what is impure will eventually come to the surface to be revealed so that it can be healed.

I invite you to partake of my light as HARIEL to engage with purity as an expression of who you truly are and how you want to live and purpose your life. Regard purification as an opportunity to 'shake off' any barnacled attitudes or actions that have dimmed your light or muffled your awareness – so that you might see the pearl that you intrinsically are ever shining at the heart of you. Amen...

4/5 * 6/19 * **9/2** * 11/14 * 1/24

16 HAKAMIAH

(ha-KA-mee-YAH)
Loyalty (G)
'One who aligns with the inner Divine'
Archangel ~ RAZIEL
Gemini / Moon (6/6-10)

I AM THAT WHICH...

helps you to reconcile the loyalties expected of you in your work with loyalty to your own true values, principles and purposes. We use the word 'reconcile' – not 'align' or 'rationalize' – because only you can decide from your own integrity how to balance loyalties to yourself personally and to your 'boss,' whether your business is your own or someone else's. Especially in consumer-based societies there is a tendency to be of 'two minds' when it comes to what is personally valued for one's self and family and the bottom line values of the business world. When the discrepancy between personal and business values is too wide, there are inevitably casualties from both sides, with hopes and dreams, well-being and integrity falling into the cracks. We know that certain paradigms underpin the structure of your economic and power-based societies, and without major cataclysms it is difficult to bring about national and global transformation of consciousness in the multitudes. However, change is still possible, one individual, family and peer group at a time. Although negative potentials and events often get the most publicity, like the turtle who wins the race with a slow steady constancy, change for the good will ultimately win out because good is the true nature of the universe, and the true nature of all beings.

The cure for 'two minds' in any work-ethic, circumstance or situation is a value system based on wholeheartedness and letting the values of the heart lead. The mind of an individual, or an organization, is a powerful data collector, computer, sorter and analyzer. It cannot, however, make the deeper connections that recognize and associate the value of what it takes in. That information comes from the intangibles of the heart – feeling, intuition, insight and wisdom. If you personally set your heart as your final decision-maker and draw on your mind's faculties for its input, as well as input from your physical needs and 'gut instincts,' then you can be one of those who begin to change the paradigm of the 'powers that be' of your world to one in which the **quantity** *of* **what** *you do and achieve is ennobled and given greater value by the* **quality** *of* **how** *it is done.*

I invite you in every two-minded moment to draw on my light as HAKAMIAH to let your heart decide. With your heart as your motivational center, your thoughts and loyalties will naturally flow toward higher principles and actions that benefit true and noble goals. When heart-truth is your first loyalty, your creativity and sense of connectedness between things and beings will enable you to formulate beneficial compromises for opposing interests and a way of integrity through impasses and impossibilities. Simply put, dear one, when you are caught 'between a rock and a hard place' of two-minds, insert heart! Amen...

September 3 – 10

Angels 17 – 24

Sephira 3

BINAH ~ Understanding

Overlighting Archangel

TZAPHKIEL ~ 'Beholder of the Divine'
Understanding of self and God, contemplation,
meditation and compassion

---

17 LAVIAH

18 CALIEL

19 LEUVIAH

20 PAHALIAH

21 NELCHAEL

22 YEIAYEL

23 MELAHEL

24 HAHEUIAH

17 LAVIAH

(LAH-vee-YAH)
Revelation (R)
'One who parts the veil'
Archangel ~ TZAPHKIEL
Gemini / Uranus (6/11-15)

I AM THAT WHICH...

helps to ease any sadness or angst of unbelonging by understanding that you are a walker of two worlds, here to give Heaven and Earth a particular experience of each other through the fullness of your own divinely-empowered human life. If you are one who sometimes feels like 'a stranger in a strange land,' know that there are many more with that feeling. Deep down in each of you, the soul misses its origin, its 'true home' – which is not your body. Your body is your 'home away from home,' a vehicle that gives your soul 'a leg to stand on' – a beautiful, highly complex 'Earthship' that collaborates with your heart, mind and soul to manifest aspects of your true soul-home in ways that can happen only on Earth. Until you understand this, you can be pulled throughout your life between a sense of displacement, yet a deep desire for meaningful place and purpose in this world. It is natural for feelings of alienation to happen when you experience loss or setbacks in your personal or work-life. Yet for many even success cannot cure existential issues because deep down there is a nagging feeling that life is about 'more than this.' And they are right.

Life IS about so much more than 'this!' And that more is found in the underneath of things and people – the meaning that gives matter mattering, the love that makes life worth living, the deeper truths held in your heart that give your being purpose. You will be susceptible to existential sadness if you look only to the outer world for meaning. Forms last only so long because the world is under the rule of time and place. You may create a legacy that lives on beyond your own life only if you have created something that is not bound by time. Something heartfelt, soulful and inspired. Something that stirs the hearts and souls of others and gives them something that keeps on giving.

So dear Earth-sojourner and walker of two worlds, I invite you to use my light as LAVIAH to part the veil of time and place to reveal a glimpse of the foreverness from which your soul was born. Together we will enter your innermost sanctum – your timeless, placeless heart – and let it wrap you in its mantle of love and truth and lead you 'behind the curtain' unto your soul where everything forgotten still remembers. Only then, when you see and feel that of Heaven which is within you, will you know what to do with your time and place on Earth. You will know that you are not here to reject this, your world, for an 'other-world,' but rather to embrace both. This is what the light of revelation is about – to see the sacred in the mundane, forever in the moment, the Divine within you and every thing and being. And to know that you are an emissary and outpost of Heaven on Earth, a feeling-thinking-highly functioning constellation of love and truth light-particles, staking a claim for what only you can become and create with your Divine-Human beingness in this privilege of time and place. Amen...

4/7 * 6/21 * **9/4** * 11/16 * 1/25

18 CALIEL

(KA-lee-EL)
Justice (S)
'One who sustains the cosmic laws of love and truth for all'
Archangel ~ TZAPHKIEL
Gemini / Saturn (6/16-21)

I AM THAT WHICH...

helps you to create your rightful place and purpose on Earth, to establish fairness and equanimity in all your dealings and to create the expansion and evolvement that your heart and soul long for. By your very existence it is meant for you to have fair opportunities to become who you truly and rightly desire to be. This cosmic truth is a constant 'law of the land:' It is your inherent birthright, privilege and soul-assumed duty and destiny to make of yourself and your life whatever you will – unfettered, unyoked and unimpeded by shame, doubt, judgment or imposition upon you by another, and also without harm to others. But then, life on Earth does not always seem just. That is why justness and justice must start and ever continue with yourself.

If you are just with yourself, then you will know how to be just with others and also be able to emerge from any seeming setback, failure or suppression unscathed on the inside. Those who cannot be just toward you will fall away – likewise seeming opportunities that do not hold your best interests will also recede. Do not mourn these, but be grateful you were spared their distraction or derailment, and look for the gift of something better on its way to you. Also, do not look for revenge or retaliation to achieve justice, for true justice is not about 'tit for tat' or 'an eye for an eye,' which are merely emotional reactions to a sense of being 'wronged.' True justice is not of this world, but rather is in the nature of the universe to 'right' itself after the forces of change have disturbed equilibrium for a time in order to expand life. True justice is about re-establishing harmony and balance based on the principles and purposes of love and truth and compassion for the needs of all. So when justice has been offended, do not look for it to be restored by the offender and do not hate the offender. By extending forgiveness and compassion, you will clear the way for justice to find its way to you from even unexpected places, and in ways that are most loving, harmonious and productive for you and all.

Thus, I invite you to draw from my light as CALIEL in those times when you are facing an unjust situation or when you are desiring to implement fair and respectful terms and conditions for any undertaking. Use my light to see that when you enter into agreements, whether contractual or verbal, the best foundation for a positive and productive working relationship is when the needs of all are considered and negotiations are aimed at all parties being treated fairly. Look at any situation through my light, as an 'angle' of love, to see the other person's 'side' and to help you create a mutually respectful collaboration. Know, dear one, however difficult some situations may seem, keeping faith with compassion, integrity, fairness and non-judgment will always bring true justice, sooner or later. Amen...

4/8 * 6/22 * **9/5** * 11/17 * 1/26

19 LEUVIAH

(LOO-vee-YAH)

Expansive Intelligence & Fruition (G)

'One who uses heart to quicken soul memory and expand mind'

Archangel ~ TZAPHKIEL

Cancer / Jupiter (6/22-26)

I AM THAT WHICH...

helps to tap the resources of your heart in order to expand your mind's capacities, reap the wisdom-fruits of knowledge and harvest the seeds of universal intelligence so that you might transform the roots of cause and effect. Expanded intelligence happens when not only the mind, but the heart is engaged. Through the insight and wisdom of the heart, you can see not only what is visibly there, but also what is there that is unseen and still forming. Or underlying factors that are affecting your visible world – whether in a negative way such as harbored hurts or unmet expectations – or a love and determination which give you and your creations a 'bigger-than-life' impact. When you see the connections and influences among things and beings in both the present and the past, and attune yourself to their separate agendas and concerns – even the need for healing – you can 'rewrite' cause and effect for an outcome that brings wholeness.

Your intelligence is informed partly by your memory. While you may accumulate a lot of data in your 'memory bank,' the memories accompanied by much emotion are those which have lasting impact on your psyche and

99

ultimately your entire being and doing. The patterns of the past and the potential future always converge in the present, and thus your power to change both the past and the future also lies in the present. You can transform the past by changing its effect on you. When you realize that all happenings in your life have been co-orchestrated by your soul and the Divine Presence within you for your healing and freedom, there is no more need for suffering. And when suffering falls away, a new vision of joy is born in which you are free to cultivate your soul purpose in the world unencumbered.

As for fruition, understand that as with anything or anyone, you can water and feed an idea or endeavor, but it must mature in its own time. Fruition happens when all the growth factors and conditions, both internal and external, are ripe. And so that the fruit does not fall on the ground and spoil, the world itself must also be ripened to the harvest – ready to receive what has been given.

Thus dear expanding and fructifying one, I offer to expand my light within you as LEUVIAH so that you might see the patterns and interconnectivity of events, ideas, encounters and beings that desire fruition. And may my light help you to discern how to nurture the newly-released seeds of every harvest. Thus may you bring forth new dynamic forms and new and productive memories of heart-mind-body-soul experience so that you might carry on, in your own unique way, the ever-present essence of the love and truth that is and has always been. Amen...

20 PAHALIAH

(pa-HA-lee-AH)
Redemption (G)
'One who restores the self'
Archangel ~ TZAPHKIEL
Cancer / Mars (6/27-7/1)

I AM THAT WHICH...

helps to bring more of your soul-self into the expression of your life so that you may know your true purpose and path, and how to course-correct self-defeating actions and attitudes in order to live in alignment with your true feelings and values. In human life, there are two aspects of you always vying for dominance: your personality-self (mind-body) and your soul-self (heart-soul). Your personality self is subject to the perks and pitfalls of short-term memory: within a short time here most of you forget that you were ever somewhere else and how Divinely light and wondrous you are underneath all that intense physical beingness! You revel in re-learning and re-experiencing the very compelling, seductive and sparkly aspects of life on Earth, and you're all about doing what you want to do, even when it hurts. Your soul-self, likewise, wants to experience life on earth too, and explore things it can do only with a body – but it hasn't forgotten who it really is or where it comes from and that it keeps alive the Divine light-spark that animates your physical self. Your soul-self also knows that all your occupations and preoccupations in this life will ultimately feel shallow and empty without the Divine meaning and mattering that your soul-purpose can give them. So the truth is that you need all your inner and outer aspects to do what you're here to do – and it is love that makes it all work.

The concepts of penance and redemption are skewed around distorted constructs of judgment and the fear of your own nature which has been indoctrinated into your psyche through the ages by dogmas and belief systems that have forgotten the ways of love. Penance is not meant to be a heavy punishing thing dragging behind you like a ball and chain or hanging over your head like a spiritual guillotine – but rather a catalyst to help you return to the love and light within your heart. For herein is the 'at-onement' with your inner Divine which enables you to redeem, as in reclaim, yourself from chaos and fragmentation and restore you to balance, harmony and lightness of being. In doing so, you become free to pursue your Divine-Human purposes and to cultivate and share the treasures of yourself with your fellow beings.

Thus I, PAHALIAH, tell you this: if you can just let all inner and outer aspects of yourself be here, working and playing in complement and co-creative exploration and expression, there will likely be little need for redeeming some 'lost' part of yourself! Enjoy the totality of who you are, for here is the only place in the universe where all that you are and can be is able to manifest. It is through you that we and all the heavens feel what it is like to be on Earth and do what can only be done here. So live and love and be true to yourself so that more and more of you might emerge and bring delight to those on the Earth and in all the other-worlds breathlessly awaiting your unfolding! Amen...

4/10 * 6/24 * **9/7** * 11/19 * 1/28

21 NELCHAEL

(NEL-ka-EL)
Ardent Desire to Learn (G)
'One who inspires delight in learning'
Archangel ~ TZAPHKIEL
Cancer / Sun (7/2-6)

I AM THAT WHICH...

helps you to draw upon the enthusiasm of the Divine within you in order to learn the true nature of things and beings, as well as how patterns and connections are intrinsically 'wired' to work together toward a unified purpose. True learning is not just about discovering something 'new,' but seeing the layers of meaning and relatedness hidden within everything. It is very easy when you are in a process of gathering knowledge and experience to be focused on the parts and not see the whole that is already there and yet always in the making, as you say, 'in the works.' But an enthusiasm for learning predisposes you to receptivity of the totality – both the seen and the unseen parts. True receptivity is not passive, but vibrant and creative. Thus, you are able to sense not only the aliveness in the parts, but also how the parts relate to each other and all else in your sphere in order to complement and expand existing patterns and connections. With this awareness you can nurture your purpose so that it becomes whole in its formation and holistic in application, bringing benefit to all.

Know also, however, that sometimes your learnings are even more profound by that which is uncreated – when things fall apart that you have been trying to put together, when plans and goals do not come to fruition, when peace and harmony have been annihilated, or hearts and bodies broken and life seemingly wasted or destroyed. These things can be your greatest teachers because of the deep effect they have on your emotions, which have the greatest teaching impact in your experiences. Here is when a desire to comprehend the meaning of things can save you from being defeated by those things. For no matter what you do or what happens in your life, if you continue to be willing to learn you will be able to re-create life and the workings of your purpose anew. Work and job titles may go away, but your purpose never leaves you because it is born of love. And love, born of the whole, is the great shapeshifter, which like water takes the shape of whatever it fills to make it whole. Thus, what you will learn finally is how to recognize love's presence in everything and everyone, and that your thirst may be quenched everywhere.

I invite you to use my light as NELCHAEL to love learning. And to know that when you are more concerned with learning than with mastery, there is no end to what will be given unto you to learn and know. May you use all that comes your way to fuel the unfolding details of your purpose to expand love and truth in your world, in your own unique ways, from your heart to another...and another. Amen...

4/11 * 6/25 * **9/8** * 11/20 * 1/29

22 YEIAYEL

(YAY-ah-YEL)
Fame, Renown (G)
'One who seeks knowing of self'
Archangel ~ TZAPHKIEL
Cancer / Venus (7/7-11)

I AM THAT WHICH...

*helps you to do what you love and love what you do for the sake of itself rather than as a means to achieve renown, and in so doing, achieve the kind of renown that comes from knowing and being truly yourself. When you work with love and enthusiasm, you are 'working your purpose,' in one way or another. The end result may be fame and recognition – but when you work for the love of it, the **quality** of your experience and the work itself will have that 'extra something' that gives you the feeling of success and true-self recognition inwardly whether outer recognition is there or not. Although your soul will try to use anything you do as a way to grow, including 'being famous for just being famous,' as you say – ultimately letting renown come as a product of being your true self is more satisfying to you at every level.*

You (the eternal soul-you) came into the human context to know and create more of yourself in a true and purposeful light. Your world offers endless venues of time, place and opportunity for individuation. As you bring more and more of your totality into expression, you share who you uniquely are with others, which ideally inspire them to do likewise, each in their own ways. No matter how attractive or talented someone else is, you are not here to be anyone but yourself – thus the only really useful part to emulate about someone else is to use their example of being who they are, to be who you are. It is prevalent in your societies to 'position,' 'market' and 'sell' yourselves and/or your works, talents and services to each other to gain recognition, fame, fortune and/or power. But when these are your primary goals, the strength and purity of your soul purposes and the ability to use your advantages in service to others can be diluted.

Not only do you and every being have a soul, but so is there a 'world soul' that is composed and shaped by the collective souls of all beings. And just like your personality-self, the world-personality becomes preoccupied with its own busyness, sparkle, seductions, hurts and challenges. But also like you, the soul of the world hungers for love, meaningful expression and beingness – and each time you offer these to the world from the love and truth of yourself, the world soul is healed a little bit more, and all around you feel it.

I invite you to draw on my light as YEIAYEL to reinvigorate meaning and purpose in your work-life and your public 'persona' in order to reflect and enlarge the person you truly are. Through the opening of your heart, you can re-purpose the use of fame as a podium for true individuation and inspiration to others to be who they truly are. You each have gifts to give, and no one is going to give them quite the way you do, with quite the same flair or flourish, kindness or humor, humility, rev or roar! Dear unique one – already famous to your Angelic audience – you can be a hole in the world, or an irreplaceable part of the whole of the world. It's your heart-call! Amen...

4/12 * 6/26 * **9/9** * 11/21 * 1/30

23 MELAHEL

(MAY-la-HEL)
Healing Capacity (G)
'One who shows where healing is possible'
Archangel ~ TZAPHKIEL
Cancer / Mercury (7/12-16)

I AM THAT WHICH...

helps you to work in a way that heals and affirms life in yourself and in whatever your purpose or path may be. Most of your life you are being called to do three things: (1) heal yourself, so that you can (2) be free to be and express more of who you truly are in your relatings and purposes, and thus (3) be a healing and encouraging presence for others to be and express who they truly are. Thus you might say that your life moves forward through cycles of healing and helping and their continual interrelatedness with each other and every aspect of your life. To that end, pain or discomfort is often your helper – an alert to get your attention. It is not meant to hurt you, but to show where healing is needed. Through healing, your fragmented and hurting parts are made whole and are able to contribute to your greater wholeness and self-unity. As you become less encumbered with personal issues, you become more present and vibrant, and therefore more available express your purpose and share your unique gifts and talents. In so doing, you can become an influence, catalyst and inspiration for others to do the same, in their own ways and 'due time.'

Healing can be facilitated from events and encounters that feel good – and also from those that don't feel so good. A healing salve can soothe a cut or an itch while doing its healing work. A hug and a kind word can comfort and create a healing energy of love and compassion. Setting a broken limb, however, may hurt as much as the break itself – but it is a productive hurt since it enables the break to heal properly. And then there's the continually irritating rub of sand in an oyster's soft tissues that yields a beautiful pearl. So it goes with the cultivation of your purposes. While seeming adversity, setback, failure, loss, disappointment, illness and so forth seem like negative events and conditions – what turns any of these into a healing catalyst is a positive and life-affirming reaction – the willingness, as your sayings go, to 'make lemonade out of lemons,' 'use the pieces to rebuild,' turn difficulties and tragedies into 'teachable moments' and the past into a more wise and noble future.

I, MELAHEL, tell you that you are 'hard-wired' at every level of your life to heal and be whole. And though you may achieve worldly glory with your work, **it is not enough for your soul that your work be glorious if you are fragmented and hurting.** *A creator is not meant to be just a conduit, but a partaker of what is brought forth – like those who teach what they need to learn, or who heal themselves while bringing healing to others. It is love that creates meaning and purpose with your work; thus endowed with love you have given your work the power to return love and meaning back to you and to create you anew. So dear one, by my love-light that is in your heart, allow the purpose within your work to re-purpose you into the one, the whole that is greater than the sum of your parts. Amen...*

4/13 * 6/27 * **9/10** * 11/22 * 1/31

24 HAHEUIAH

(ha-HOO-ee-YAH)
Protection (G)
'One who is the keeper of true-selfness'
Archangel ~ TZAPHKIEL
Cancer / Moon (7/17-22)

I AM THAT WHICH...

helps to guide you toward people, opportunities and work that feed your true purposes, and to protect you from the seeming harm of adverse events, circumstances or inner impediments by using them for your learning and becoming. You are here on Earth to experiment, explore and create – and there are opportunities to define and refine your potential and purposes in both positive and seemingly negative experiences. Falling down is an opportunity to exercise your 'standing-back-up' muscles. Hitting a wall now and then helps you to learn how to walk around, over or through impediments. Encountering obstacles can teach you how to transform anything that stands in your way into a way of opportunity. So without purposeful harm to yourself or another, please do try different things and ways that you are drawn to! If you should 'cross a line,' rely on your built-in natural 'pangs' of conscience to help you quickly set right the offense so that you are not derailed into a swamp of continuing self-remorse and recrimination. Self-judgment only results in self-suppression – so don't let it be a life sentence that prohibits you from true 'at-onement'!

Your willingness to set something right activates the light of Love and Truth within you, which are always your greatest protectors and advocates. These are the fabric and nature of the Universe and your very own being, and thus can never be vanquished or prevailed against – however much darkness you may seem to suffer before the light of day is yours again. The saving graces of Love and Truth always dangle as an intertwined lifeline in your heart of hearts like the ripcord of a parachute. Use my protective light as HAHEUIAH to illuminate the possibility to pull on it before you ever have to hit bottom!

As your purpose and work evolve and align, call on my protection and inner guidance to help continually calibrate your choices and actions with the values you hold dear and which reflect who you truly are. It is very easy when working for other people and entities to be drawn into their visions, purposes and bottom lines. We would wish for you to never choose work based solely on the need to gain money – but if you feel that is necessary at times in your life, then we say to transform your work by bringing to it the quality of your own inner purposes. When you do the most menial, 'foreign' or distasteful tasks with heart – meaning willingness, integrity and care – you ennoble yourself and the work. Disrespect the work and you disrespect yourself by association. Your best interests and best outcomes are always protected by whole-heartedness and respect. And if a job or work is lost to you, know that we are helping to protect you and your true purposes from where you do not belong. So do not be blinded by the darkness behind you, but look ahead with your heart at the light that is ever inviting you forward. Amen...

September 11 – 18

Angels 25 – 32

Sephira 4

CHESED ~ Love/Mercy

Overlighting Archangel

TZADKIEL ~ 'Justice of God'
Mercy and kindness, beneficence,
grace, transmutation

---

25 NITH-HAIAH

26 HAAIAH

27 YERATEL

28 SEHEIAH

29 REIYEL

30 OMAEL

31 LECABEL

32 VASARIAH

25 NITHAIAH

(NIT-ha-YAH)
Spiritual Wisdom and Magic (R)
'One who quickens the abracadabra of life'
Archangel ~ TZADKIEL
Leo / Uranus (7/23-27)

I AM THAT WHICH...

helps you to cultivate spiritual wisdom into a magical life full of presence and purpose by using your dreams and meditations to stimulate deeper soul work, heart-awakening, inspiration and a greater awareness of patterns and interconnections. The first step toward a magical life is in realizing that there is more to it than meets the eye. Dreams, meditations, inner visions and communications remind you of this and can give you timely clues and guidances to help you connect outer challenges and opportunities with the need for inner healing and 'truing-up.' Thus may your 'magical powers' may be unleashed! Inspiration brings about the 'in-spiriting' of a greater potential through love as creation energy, making you feel magical, connected – and possible. Ultimately, the hub that connects all connections and creates that magical feeling of 'more' is your heart, which is the broadcaster of your soul.

When we speak of your heart, we mean your sacred heart – the loving, insightful and wise 'wholistic' locus where the Human and the Divine meet within you, connecting you to the powers of Heaven and the opportunities of Earth. Just

*as your physical heart-organ is the central hub for the in-
and-out flow of your vital lifeblood and the bio-intelligence
which translates emotions into thought and physical
response – your sacred heart, with its powers of feeling,
knowing and wisdom-making, is your Divine 'master organ'
which informs and expands the faculties of your mind and
helps to make meaningful sense out of accumulated
knowledge and experience.*

*As a Divine-Human interface, your sacred heart is the
broadcaster of your soul, conveyed to your humanity as an
inner voice of love and truth, intuition and the desire for
meaning and purpose. Through your soul-infused heart, you
are able to transcend the seeming limitations of time and
place and have an 'all-access pass' to the eternal and the all-
knowing, all-being and all-oneness which can amplify your
experiences and expressions on Earth. Through a soul-
empowered heart, love and compassion for self and others is
deepened and heightened, and you are able to use meaning
and purpose to create magic in even the seeming mundane
and routine of life.*

*Thus, dear one who seeks a magical life, I invite you to
use my light-energy as NITHAIAH to shine a light of
revelation upon your dreams and inner receivings as
signposts upon your heart-path. Sometimes in human life
the longest distance is to the nearest destination. You may
often stumble in the paradox of seeking and finding forever
in the here and now – and yourself – not in the cacophony of
the world, but in the cradle of your own sacred heart. To
find the magic of life, you must come to know that YOU are
the magic of life. And my eternal light-calling is to illuminate
that loving truth of you. Amen...*

4/15 * 6/29 * **9/12** * 11/24 * 2/2

26 HAAIAH

(HA-ee-YAH)
Political Science and Ambition (R)
'One who encourages cooperative expression'
Archangel ~ TZADKIEL
Leo / Saturn (7/28-8/1)

I AM THAT WHICH...

helps to modulate excessive impulses of desire and thought so that you are balanced, healthy and free to pursue your higher truths and purposes. Every human being is composed of an inner (soul-self) and outer (personality-self), which are bridged by the dynamics of the heart-mind 'matrix.' Often soul and personality have opposing agendas, but the 'game of life' is about your soul's ambition to grow, experience and learn by manifesting more and more of itself through your personality expressions. In the soul's corner is your heart, and in personality's corner is your mind. The 'political order' that is most beneficial to your total well-being and fulfillment, as well as your contribution to society, is one in which your heart-soul is the visionary 'executive branch,' with your mind-personality as the delegated 'worker' branch. When you are 'out of order,' you are literally and cosmically just that. Your internal ruling order is askew, either as a cause or effect of imbalanced and rampant emotions, urges or influences, which create inner anarchy and mayhem and hold you and your purposes hostage to emotional turmoil. This is, as you say, 'no way to live.'

When your soul comes into Earth-life, its memories and purposes become dimmed in the denser vibrations and survival needs of physical beingness, as well as the attraction to matter, both the perks and pitfalls of free will and the general tendency of your lighter Divine nature to be submerged and muffled by your heavier human nature. This is why we Angelic 'angles' of light consciousness have been given to dwell within and among you – to lighten you with our light by reminding you of your own. It is so much easier to see what is important if what you are looking at is well lit!

Thus, you are gently and lovingly invited to use my light as HAAIAH to magnify your own light so that you might see what is most important, valuable and true for the whole of you. In certain of your holy scriptures you are invited to look first to God and all things will be added unto you from there. These are different words for all we are saying here – look first to the light of love and truth that you may see the reflection of your whole self therein. And then see what it is that you truly want based on who you truly are, a child of light, a carrier and broadcaster of light, a unique ray of magnificence which has come to lighten the body and being that has so kindly consented to give you the opportunity to 'touch down' on this privilege of Earth. Be the light you are, dear one, and bring your shining to the world which needs you. Amen...

4/16 + 17am * 6/30 * **9/13** * 11/25 * 2/3

27 YERATEL

(YEH-ra-TEL)
Propagation of the Light (S)
'One who grows the light with love'
Archangel ~ TZADKIEL
Leo / Jupiter (8/2-6)

I AM THAT WHICH...

helps to bring the light seeds of consciousness within you into fruition so that the Divine Light might be harvested and continually regenerated in your humanity. Thereby your purposes may be ennobled and the light of the Heavens dispersed through you and all your doings. Light seeds hold bits of cosmic information about who you are, your soul purpose and a kind of 'ignition switch' for igniting your Divine soul-spark into an eternal flame of love and truth in your heart. As Truth is the certainty of your particular' isness' within the Divine 'I Am,' Love is that which will grow and make of the Truth that you are all you desire to become. As the love and truth of your Divine-Human beingness is rooted in time and place on Earth, you will become as a lighted candle – standing strong and vibrant in your own light, adding your light to that of others, and even helping to ignite the sleeping embers within other human hearts.

You might think of the moments when you are 'fired' into higher-consciousness as those moments when you are awakened – as in the image rendered by your artists again and again since its first depiction as the hand of God reaching to touch the hand of man. In that image, man's hand is languid like that of a sleeper, as yet unaware of the Divine reaching toward him to ignite the cosmic spark of soul-light which will animate his physicality. While you may have a profound first moment of awakening that cracks you open to the light inside, you will likely experience many awakening moments throughout your life – for the denser energies of life will now and then seem to lull you to sleep. Except once awakened, your times of sleep will be as an early dawn or a twilight that never quite goes dark.

As you journey through each day, may you be conscious of what you bring into every space you enter – whether it be in your own or someone else's home or workplace, or the space of another person's heart, mind or body. Do you bring something of yourself which will increase the light, or dim it? Light is fluid, so if you are finding yours a bit dim in a moment, use your inner 'dimmer switch' to take it up!

Therefore, dear lighted one, I offer you my light-energy as YERATEL to keep your light lit so that the life-fire within you may spring forth again and again in that timeless place between soul and physicality which is your sacred heart. Here is where the Divine Spark of your soul has become a flame that shall never die as long as you live and beyond. Here is where you become aware and responsive to the needs, desires and purposes of your unique aliveness, and ultimately, how your aliveness may enliven and contribute to the light and life of the world. Together we shall grow and expand the light that you are, the light you desire to become, the light you have always been and ever will be. Amen...

4/17pm + 18 * 7/1 * **9/14** * 11/26 * 2/4

28 SEHEIAH

(say-HAY-ee-YAH)
Longevity (G)
'One who extends life with creation energy'
Archangel ~ TZADKIEL
Leo / Mars (8/7-12)

I AM THAT WHICH...

helps to foster vitality and creative living through the continual balancing of ideas/inspiration (Fire), emotions/ flow (Water) and manifestation (Earth). In nature, when fire and water come into unity, they seem to extinguish each other; however, from the perspective of the ongoingness of creation, their mergence actually brings about a third thing – steam, which then unites with the atmosphere as air. Your thoughts, ideas and emotions are meant to work together toward manifestation; however, they must each have a place and purpose within you without overcoming or annihilating any other aspect. Equilibrium is achieved not by suppressing one or the other, but by each part helping to define and facilitate the other so that they can perform individually, and thus together, at a higher level. In this way, what is created is something more than the sum of the parts – something that no one part could have created or become without the others. For example, a good idea gives the emotions subject matter and focus, and the feeling and passion for that idea sparks the firing of more ideas, inspiration and creative flow so that manifestation can occur. It is this combination that gives longevity to great works of art. The feeling and inspiration that created them continues to vibrate within them and is transmitted to whoever is drawn to them, even centuries later.

Of all the influences which bring about the actualizing of inspirations and ideas into matter, it is great feeling – in a word, love – that most engenders longevity. When you put love into your work, whatever that work is, you create an atmosphere of nobility and integrity within and around it which radiates out to others. Love attracts and creates more of itself through expansion and plenitude, as any enthusiastic green-thumbed gardener knows. When the leaders of projects and companies operate with higher motivations and respect for all, it is evident throughout the organization at every level. Even the most menial job, when done with care and consideration, is noticeable and impactful.

Thus, I, SEHEIAH, invite you to draw on my eternal light-energy to stretch time by doing what you love and loving what you do. Love is life's creation energy, and as such is the generator of foreverness! Consider in your life what enjoyments you partake of, even if only occasionally, that give you a sense of timelessness – and do them more often. For the more timelessness you bring to time, the more of life you will have within time. And herein, dear eternal one, is your personal 'anti-aging' formula for continual renewal, well-being and longevity! Amen...

4/19 * 7/2 * **9/15** * 11/27 * 2/5

29 REIYEL

(RAY-ee-YEL)

Liberation (G)

'One who liberates the Love and Truth of you'

Archangel ~ TZADKIEL

Leo / Sun (8/13-17)

I AM THAT WHICH...

helps to free you from emotions, thoughts and beliefs that dim the light-being of love and truth which you essentially are and which your soul longs to express and give purpose to within your humanity. You are here to become free from the 'karma' of unresolved and unhealed issues so that you may proceed unencumbered toward the 'dharma' of your soul purposes on Earth. When you are weighed down by unresolved personal pain and conflict, you are not fully available to the unfolding of your greater purposes, nor are your gifts fully available to be developed and offered in service to the world.

Furthermore, if you would truly allow truth to 'set you free,' then you must follow it beyond what you have previously thought to be true whenever love calls you to do so. Anything that you fear, doubt, claim, believe, feel, think, do or own can undermine you if it prevents the evolution and expansion of your consciousness and the fullness of your feeling and experience. Love's truth does not divide and separate or exclude. Beliefs, dogmas and traditions are languages about particular perceptions of truth, and paths by which you may explore and explain it – but these are not Truth itself. The whole Truth can only be known in the company of Love, which sees not only who you are here and now in time, but also what more you are that you have not yet manifested. Your eternal soul-self longs to be expressed through your heart, mind and body in this unique life experience that you have chosen. When you allow Truth to set you free, in so doing you set Truth itself free to evolve into new truths that expand your life and create more space for more of you to be revealed and expressed.

So dear truth-and-freedom seeker, use my light as REIYEL to illuminate and dispel any dark and tight 'nooks and crannies' within you – and to unleash the fire of love held in your heart for the soul-purpose blazing within it. Allow my light to expand within you in order to liberate the soul of you ever longing to be manifested. And know that as you become free, so do you free us, your Angelic heart-dwellers, to shine forth as the true and eternal you, fully alive, fully human as an expression of the Divine manifesting on Earth. Amen...

4/20 * 7/3 * **9/16** * 11/28 * 2/6

30 OMAEL

(O-ma-EL)
Fertility, Multiplicity (G)
'One who loves life into being'
Archangel ~ TZADKIEL
Leo / Venus (8/18-22)

I AM THAT WHICH...

brings creativity, support and proliferation to ideas, enterprises and undertakings where the love and truth of you is vibrant and motivational to your purposes. There is no endeavor or success more fertile and prolific than that which is brought into being by the creation energy of love with the rootedness and guidance of truth. Wherever there is love, truth attends so that the thing which is created may be manifested as a true 'isness' unto itself. And wherever there is truth, love brings the ability to 'go forth and multiply.' This is what is happening when a poem, a song, a work of art or any endeavor, project – or offspring – seems to 'take on a life of its own,' as it increases the energies of its own beingness and spawns new life, ideas and creations. You might say that truth is the seed, and love is the fertilizer. Truth provides integrity of structure and the way and means for existence to be manifested, while Love provides the spirit, the fire, the passion and commitment that inspires, energizes and ultimately multiplies beingness. Together in their love-and-truth forged 'kiln of creation,' new life is shaped, fired and shared for the increase of itself and the world.

All seed plantings look forward to the harvest, and it is a cosmic law as true in the cosmos as it is upon Earth and in the humus of every soul and soil where seeds are sown for new creations: 'whatsoever you sow shall you reap.' You cannot put a thorn in the ground and expect it to come up as a rose. If your harvest is disappointing, look back to examine – from which part of yourself did you plant the seeds of your endeavors? What were your motivations? Did you respect and attend lovingly to that which you brought into creation, or were you just going through the motions? It is important for you to know that living energies, even seemingly inanimate objects and ideas, inherently respond to the presence or absence of the energy of love – in much the same way you lean in toward a caress or back away from a slap, even if you are only observing those actions of others. Even disinterest or negligence is felt as an absence of love – whereas, you and all things and beings are hard-wired to proliferate and shine in the presence of love's welcoming attention, acceptance and encouragement! This is why, as most gardeners and 'success-against-all-oddsters' know, that even with a poor start, where there is introduced even one "iota" of love and nurturing, conditions and circumstances can be transformed into fertile influences and opportunities.

Therefore, I OMAEL, encourage you dear host and outpost of the Divine Love and Truth on Earth: whatever your personal situation, work, projects or purposes – bring them love and you will create something true with the power to bring forth new life within you and all who engage with it. Amen...

4/21 * 7/4 + 5am * **9/17** * 11/29 * 2/7

31 LECABEL

(LAY-ka-BEL)
Intellectual Talent (G)
'One who puts all the pieces together'
Archangel ~ TZADKIEL
Virgo / Mercury (8/23-28)

I AM THAT WHICH...

acts as a muse for the visionary and problem-solver by helping to combine mental acuity with creative intuition and sustained enthusiasm for initiating innovative ideas and carrying them forward into timely implementation and fruition. Feeling and the creativity it inspires are tremendously important to the early stages of projects and processes. When you are impassioned with an idea, dream or goal, it is often your great feeling for it that not only gets you started with something remarkable and unique, but puts you far enough down the road that there is 'no turning back' when the way gets bumpy and the destination is not yet in sight. What is also needed, however, are strategies, implementation and plans of action for forward movement. Thus, you might say that a really powerful and innovative 'train of thought' needs not only a creative engine (heart), but also a supportive caboose (head) and track to go the distance (feet)! With heart, head and feet, your work becomes meaningful, strategic and productive.

When head and heart are working together, you are better able to discern the workings of things through their components, seasons, cycles and patterns. You can see and feel their interconnections and their potential for beneficial dynamics among the parts as well as toward the unity of the whole. Indeed, it is when the deeper wisdom and discernment of heart is introduced that 'mere' mental intelligence becomes intellectual talent – giving your mind a far vaster reach than when it tries to work on its own. In this way, when you are ready for action, your effort can seem almost effortless because you are 'working smart.' You come to know how to utilize and amplify positive potential at the best time for ripening and flow – and problems, obstacles or setbacks are not seen as such, but rather as opportunities for creative reassessment, exploring new directions or infusing new 'lifeblood.'

Thus, dear aspiring and purposeful one, I invite you to use my muse-light as LECABEL to light your remarkable and unique way in order to work your purpose and purpose your work. When you understand your own diverse parts as vital assets that compose your own whole, you will more easily discern how to optimize all the different parts of your work toward a unified goal. Working smart – with both head and heart – you will surely bring more visible light into the world and inspire the conscious and creative purposefulness of others. Amen...

4/22 * 7/5pm + 6 * **9/18** * 11/30 * 2/8

32 VASARIAH

(va-SAH-ree-YAH)
Clemency and Equilibrium (G)
'One who balances judgment with mercy'
Archangel ~ TZADKIEL
Virgo / Moon (8/29-9/2)

I AM THAT WHICH...

*helps you to continually forgive and let go of the disappointments and ebbs of life so that they may naturally pass and make room for a new incoming flow. In order for new creations and a new state of harmony, balance and well-being to emerge, old ways and beingness must fall away. As you are working your purpose and purposing your work in life, you are subject to the natural in-and-out, ebb-and-flow movements of life. The tide comes in and brings nourishment, gifts, opportunities, successes and all manner of abundance. Then the tide goes out and takes with it what is no longer needed (however attached you might have become to it) in order to create space for the new gifts and surprises that will be borne on the next incoming tide. The comings and goings of life's details continually renew the canvas of your life – like when the seashore's receding waves take with them all the flotsam, miscellany and markings made by things and beings, leaving behind a smooth-surfaced sand ready for new footprints and sandcastles. Forgiving the passing of 'what was' is **for giving** 'what will be' time and place for its emergence.*

In societies where the destination is more prized than the journey and the quantity of success more revered than the quality, it can be hard to forgive and not rue, cry and hue over seeming setbacks and failures. But dear one you do not learn nearly as much from your successes as you do from your setbacks, and the sooner you embrace them the sooner you can see their opportunities and gifts. Setbacks give you the chance to set yourself back a little from your trajectory to reevaluate, broaden your perspective and perhaps bring back into balance an area that was becoming contrived, forced or skewed in some way while you were mono-focused on success.

So dear striving one, please feel free to fashion my VASARIAH energy into a 'light-balancing pole' to help you ride the fluctuations of your incomings and outgoings and see them both as opportunities. For indeed, life is like a 'balancing beam,' and just like the tightrope walker you should not wait till you get to the other side of the chasm to start balancing your movements. You must keep balancing and re-balancing as you go or you will never get to the other side – the feat-accomplished side – still on your feet! Amen...

September 19 – 27

Angels 33 – 40

Sephira 5

GEBURAH ~ Strength & Judgment

Overlighting Archangel

CHAMAEL ~ 'Severity of God'
(Also CHAMUEL or KAMAEL)
Change, purification and clearing of karma
for stronger loving and nurturing relationships

---

33 YEHUIAH

34 LEHAHIAH

35 CHAVAKIAH

36 MENADEL

37 ANIEL

38 HAAMIAH

39 REHAEL

40 YEIAZEL

33 YEHUIAH

(vay-HOO-ee-YAH)
Subordination to Higher Order (R)
'One who calls you to higher ground'
Archangel ~ CHAMAEL
Virgo / Uranus (9/3-7)

I AM THAT WHICH...

helps you to discern value and to prioritize the order of things and rightful place in that order according to what truly matters, and to allow priorities to change as core values call for a different focus. Priorities are often built with structure, and anything structural – whether a building or a plan 'set in stone' – tends to be rigid. Therefore, in the way some structures are built with moveable engineering to withstand extremely windy and earthquake-prone areas, you must build your structures with bendable components in order to meet the ever-changing circumstances of life. 'Building in' fluidity to those things that are fixed by their very nature, including the concept of certainty itself, allows you and your endeavors to keep going and not 'fall apart' even when everything is changing. And even while changes may totally disrupt the order you had organized, if you can maintain or reconnect with what is most important first – then you will be able to re-create new forms and structures around that.

So then, in order to know what you value most about any endeavor, I, YEHUIAH, invite you to ask and answer this one question in whatever you do and dream: 'why?' When your why is sincere and motivated by a higher-ground perspective, then the 'how' will reveal itself. And, you will be able to change the how if the ground should turn into shifting sands – and still hold true to your why. Not that the why won't sometimes change as well and become so much more than you imagined – for example the person who 'chucks it all' to go off to some nether-region of the world to 'find himself,' only to find purpose and place helping what you call a 'third-world' village to build a school or create a water system. There is only one thing that has this kind of fluidity and yet can still remain constant, moreso than even the waters of the ocean – and that is love.

When love is the why in your work, then your work becomes your purpose and your purpose your work. And even as your work may change, your purpose will remain and keep evolving. When love is your highest order, and all else is 'subordinate' to that, then you can regard change, upheaval and seeming obstacles as inspirational motivators – not setbacks or failures. To love is the soul's success, and the greatest dreams and doings cannot hold a candle to love's light. Thus, my light as YEHUIAH wishes this for you above all else and after all is said and done in your life – that you may be able to chronicle, as the song says, 'what I did for love.' Amen...

4/24 * 7/8 * **9/20** + **21**am * 12/2 * 2/10

34 LEHAHIAH

(lay-HA-hee-YAH)
Obedience (R)
'One who amplifies inner authority'
Archangel ~ CHAMAEL
Virgo / Saturn (9/8-12)

I AM THAT WHICH...

helps you to respect and obey the natural laws of seasons and self-sovereignty for the manifestation in due time of your particular purposes, by understanding that each thing and being has an inner authority according to its own unique nature and way of manifesting. The leaf of a tree turns into the light in obedience to its nature and need for light, while the trunk is sturdy and bends only to great winds. Love is fluid and pervasive, and like water, takes the shape of whatever it fills. While truth seeks manifestation and rootedness, its nature is both absolute and relative and thus expresses an aspect of itself through the language and forms of each who undertake it. All living things and beings seek purpose, but each shall work their purpose in unique ways, times and places according to their nature – unless their nature is interfered with.

In a natural childbirth, the child chooses its own time of emergence according to the nature and environment of its physicality and its soul-urge. An artist obeys his nature to make art – but if he is too oppressed by the world's demands and responsibilities and thus constrained to work at something else, he may suffer and lose sovereignty of self and his art. The same is true for any who are called to a particular expression without the apparent means to obey that call. And then, there are those who enjoy many kinds of work and find their purpose in how they do what they do rather than what. No one way fits all, because you are here to do it your way as an expression of a particular aspect of the Divine on Earth – and you are the only one who can!

The truths of humankind have been portrayed in as many umpteen billion diverse ways as there have existed beings since the beginning of Creation. Love, however, which lives in the hearts of each and all, tells about the sameness of humankind on the inside. And at the core of that sameness is the call to obey your inner authority, the Divine that dwells within you, through you and as you in a co-creation that is utterly unique to your Divine-Human beingness.

Therefore, my light as LEHAHIAH is given unto you to amplify your own inner authority for the cultivation and expression of your unique being. Be not utterly disappointed or discouraged when circumstances seem to prevent the fulfillment of your desires. Trust the authority within and know that all things in the unseen worlds are working for the highest good of yourself and all the aspects and aspirations of you which are still in formation. Do not force or contrive yourself or your desires. Come to understand your nature and the nature of that which you aspire to. If there is anything in this or other worlds which would hurry time, it is only this: love. Love what you want, and it will quicken because in Love's love for you, all that is done unto you will be for the manifestation of your soul-truth in time and place on this Earth. Amen...

4/25 * 7/9 * **9/21**pm + **22** * 12/3 * 2/11

35 CHAVAKIAH

(cha-VA-kee-YAH)

Reconciliation (R)

'One who resolves paradox'

Archangel ~ CHAMAEL

Virgo / Jupiter (9/13-17)

I AM THAT WHICH...

helps you to reconcile and balance what you are called to inwardly with what physicality and the outer world seems to demand of you, and to reform any thoughts about what you 'should' be or do as compared to what you truly want to do. You are here on this Earth to do what you truly want, from the bottom of your soul to the highest peak of your heart, together with the potential vastness of your mind. That's what you naturally do, to a large extent, when part of you is 'out of body' and 'other-worldly' – which is reflected in your imagination, fantasies and creativities. However, there is quite a lot of stuff you can't do without a body! So your soul came here to 'up the ante' – to materialize your soul-aspirations in time and space in a way that can only be done here. The catch, however, is that physicality subjects you to forgetting what it is you came here to do! And when you remember, you will have to do it within the much denser vibrations of flesh and bone, linear time and particular place – the soul's version of trying to fly through mud. And this is why we Angels so marvel at how brave, adventurous and stubbornly determined you are as Divine-Human beings!

So, like it or not, you have got to use your in-born, on-board creativity to reconcile your inner with your outer and your soul-essence with your personality-expression, so that you can take on the journey of life with your heart in full throttle. In order to do this, you must first accept that both worlds, the seen and the unseen, are valid and important to who and where you are and what you want to do. On Earth, the 'starving artist' must eat or he will leave behind fewer paintings. In approaching your whole life as an art form, you can have it all – rather than sacrificing one part for the other. **The key to this is accepting that your privilege and purpose on Earth is to express and fulfill the truth of yourself – and then use your creativity to organize everything else around that.** Even if you have a family to support, imagine how the atmosphere in your family would change if this spiritually higher standard of living became the bottom line for every member of the family – so that all work together to help each other cultivate their personal best while ensuring that all outer needs are also being met.

And so, I, CHAVAKIAH, impart unto you an important tip: you can only do this with love enough, for love is the creation energy of the universe. Love yourself, each other and the thing you aspire to that is an expression, and an exploration, of your heart-and-soul truth. Bring everything you think you know, every experience, every need, every demand, every challenge and responsibility to your heart, and your heart will show you how to reconcile them to each other through inclusivity. Bring love, and love will transform anything into a golden opportunity for a richer, wiser, more potent and purposeful life. Amen...

4/26 * 7/10 * **9/23** * 12/4 * 2/12

36 MENADEL

(MEH-na-DEL)
Inner/Outer Work (S)
'One who dances two worlds into one'
Archangel ~ CHAMAEL
Virgo / Mars (9/18-23)

I AM THAT WHICH...

helps you to develop an outer work that allows you to manifest your inner calling and utilize the innate talents, skills and natural interests which reflect your soul purposes and potentials. Any work in which you are engaged with enthusiasm and a sense of meaning and purpose is inspiring and energizing, and you can choose to bring these qualities of experience to whatever work you do. There may be times when your purpose is not so much about your job description, but about cultivating new skills, character and collaborations, or developing connections with certain colleagues in preparation for future prospects. Sometimes you are at a particular job to help you know more about what you don't want to do or how you don't want to be treated. In an ideal world, we would wish for you to never have to take a job only for the paycheck – especially if that job brings you disrespect or unappreciation. But even if there are aspects of your work which would diminish you, any work done with self-respect, care and dignity dignifies and expands you and your soul purposes.

When you are engaged with your innate creativity and true aspirations, jobs or projects are venues and stepping stones for the growth and harvest of your potential and your unfolding as a Divine-Human being. Should that potential become stymied or stale because of poor conditions, ethics, attitudes or unproductive endeavors, it's time to either move up or move on. Moving up doesn't necessarily mean a 'job promotion.' It can also be about reinventing your job – changing, adding or taking away certain tasks, changing where you work or who you work with. Any change that deepens a sense of purpose and creates a rise in your enjoyment and enthusiasm is 'moving up' in our Angelic book! All that said, we understand that at times you may have to do whatever job you can find in order to support other responsibilities or endeavors that are important to you. However, consider that a prolonged time doing any job you dislike or which is toxic to you on any level, even for the noblest reasons, can eat away at your health and happiness.

While your outer could likely do any kind of job, your inner is always seeking the expression of purpose. Your outer might like to 'get rich quick,' but your inner wants to experience the ongoing richness of a meaningful life. Your inner work is always to make sense of and ennoble your outer work, while your outer work is to make sure your inner is being manifested into fruitful action. Thus, dear deserving one, I invite you to use my light as MENADEL to help you to remember and reclaim the importance of what you love and that you are entitled to do right and true work. Thereby may you acquire the greater treasures of life wrought through the continual collaboration of your inner and outer in all your purposes and endeavors! Amen...

37 ANIEL

(AH-nee-EL)
Breaking the Circle (G)
'One who lifts you out of the circle into the light'
Archangel ~ CHAMAEL
Libra / Sun (9/24-28)

I AM THAT WHICH...

helps to raise your sights into bigger-picture perspectives in order to open up new avenues of opportunity and break out of 'old ways of working' which keep exercising the same unproductive strategies in new scenarios. Are you a 'Sisyphus,' ever rolling the rock up the hill, only to have it roll back down near the top and have you running down to push it back up again...and again? I, ANIEL, say to you ever so respectfully, you cannot break this pattern by finding a new or better rock. You must change the thinking that says you have to keep pushing the rock up the hill, or you will be captive to a relentless cycle of your own making between the bottom and near-top of the hill. This kind of thinking might have been learned early on as a survival modality or as a continual act of will against obstacles standing in your way. And though pushing the rock up the hill may have once helped you to develop determination and stamina 'against all odds' – this can get carried beyond its usefulness into a pattern of stubbornness and fear-based habit. Furthermore, you can do this your whole life and not be aware that you're doing the same thing over and over, or getting the same results again and again – or that your life is getting harder and harder. As you get harder and harder.

For the problem with pushing rocks up hills is that you become the resistance that the rock is always pushing against, since all it wants to do is obey the law of gravity, i.e., the path of least resistance, and roll to a level place. And so you will keep fighting a battle that cannot be won – unless you unshoulder the burden, step off the path that has become a rut, and let the rock roll down. Consider that if you aim for the sky of your heart rather than the top of the hill, you will be able to access the inspiration and quantum creativity that can 'fly' you to any hilltop you desire! Following your heart above all else will ultimately put your feet on a path that is natural and has its own kind of momentum – which will sometimes even carry YOU.

A paradox of living is that life expands and moves itself forward in circles – as in the seasons and cycles of nature and physicality. However, these circles are ever widening, deepening and rising, because the circles of life move as spirals. They never traverse the exact same terrain, but rather circle around and beyond it. Perhaps you take the same route to work every day – but if you broaden your perspective enroute to become more aware of what's around you – then you have lifted yourself out of the circle of sameness into a new terrain of discovery. Then you start "riding" the spiral of life and the flow of momentum. This is how life and all beings are expanded, within your own lifetime and from one generation to another, and with the Divine Itself and all the worlds seen and unseen. So let us, you and I who am ANIEL, spend the rest of your life together breaking circles and spreading wings! Amen...

4/28 * 7/12 * **9/25** * 12/6 * 2/14

38 HAAMIAH

(ha-AH-mee-YAH)
Ritual and Ceremony (G)
'One who enlivens the path with love'
Archangel ~ CHAMAEL
Libra / Venus (9/29-10/3)

I AM THAT WHICH...

helps you to cultivate heart-centered spiritual practice so that your inner is manifested outwardly in ways that stimulate the true and noble potential of all you do and create. Thus, intuition and will become initiative and willingness, wisdom and understanding become sensitivity and compassion, soul identity becomes meaningful purpose, intelligence expands into higher consciousness, thought becomes noble expression, and inspiration and creativity bring forth love-and-life-affirming forms. A heart-centered spiritual practice is one in which your most sacred altar is your own heart, the place where you meet the Divine within to bow down and rise up in the particularities of love and truth that are yours to receive and give. At this innermost altar you are called to come not only as you are, but also who you long to be. Here you are ordained into the rites of your own becoming – for your own great joy of being, and to cultivate the treasures to be given unto others from the ever-increasing love and truth of yourself. Simply put, your heart becomes your way – the practice of why and how in whatever you do. The purpose in your work. The motivation

141

in your motor. The higher calling of your bottom line. Your beginning and end game.

While meditational practices often focus on silencing the mind – the mind, like a small child, will resist being silenced. In these mind-resistant moments come into your heart, softly and deeper within to the timeless-placelessness that was and is before words were born. Kneel down at this innermost altar...be still and know the I Am within you that is the miracle of you, the urge and impetus of you and your reason for being. Pray the embracing prayer of I-AMness. And then go out into the world from this heart-communion so that you may give from the miracle of your own being, and receive the miracle of others and the glories of their contributions. See that there is purpose for everyone. Purpose for you. Purpose for all there is.

Only your own heart knows your particular purpose, for your heart is the lover and confidant of your soul. Thus, purpose is a revelation of your soul unto your heart, according to your readiness and willingness. So be not discouraged, dear one, if your purpose at any time in your life is not yet in your consciousness. Allow me to help you to cultivate the ritual of coming unto your heart, in stillness and trust, to await the answers to your questions of longing and desire, knowing that it is the answer within you desiring to be known which has given you the question. Let the inner path become well-worn. Use your heart as your personal true-north, the inner home-star by which you may always be found, and my light will be as wings to carry you there, again and again. Amen...

4/29 * 7/13 * **9/26** * 12/7 * 2/15

39 REHAEL

(RAY-ha-EL)
Filial Submission (G)
'One who honors what was while inspiring what will be'
Archangel ~ CHAMAEL
Libra / Mercury (10/4-8)

I AM THAT WHICH...

helps you to balance what is needed for work goals and protocols with your own values and purposes so that profitability benefits not only business success but personal integrity and fulfillment. Whether you work at your own business, provide a service or work for an organization or government agency, you are called upon to respect the 'higher-ups' and the goals of that business. When it's your own business, you – and your partners, if any – are the obvious higher-ups, and you set not only the goals and purposes of your business, but how you go about achieving them. In this scenario, there is choice available to you at every moment of decision-making, though the needs and demands of clients and customers can sometimes make you feel otherwise. Ideally, you are constantly learning from past performances and results as you weigh bigger-picture factors with the pieces of the puzzle that are needed to fill in that picture. When quality and integrity are part of your bottom line, you can periodically review and re-align business and personal values so that they are in harmony and mutually supportive. While you may work many more

143

hours in your own business, if you continually exercise choice you will always be the captain of your ship, the parent of your creation. The point is to own your own business, not have your business own you. Working for others, however, is a trickier business!

*Acknowledging the importance to you of a paycheck, it helps (1) to work in an environment where there is mutual respect, communication and collaboration from the top down and the bottom up; (2) to actually like/admire/ appreciate the services and products that the organization provides; and (3) that the 'means to the end' – protocols and procedures – practice values that you can agree with. Alas, more often than not, the scenario is very different. However, unless you want and are willing to create or find different and better work, then you must find your own way of working within an imperfect setting that does not offend your personal values. Rather than conforming to lower standards, be the presence that infuses a more integritous work ethic. And you don't have to convert others – start by just being that yourself. This is how you transform work that seems to go against your purpose into work that IS your purpose – by **how** you work. Even when you're required to follow specific procedures, it is your choice to do your tasks with love, respect and harmonious cooperation.*

I, REHAEL, lovingly assure you that your actions will have impact. Yes, you may get fired, or you may quit. Or you may be hired into a higher position by some higher-up who's been noticing your extra efforts. Or you may start your own business, doing things your own way. Whatever you do, be the child of your own heart and you will win, because the integrity of love and truth never loses. Amen...

4/30 * 7/14 * **9/27** * 12/8 * 2/16

40 YEIAZEL

(YAY-ah-ZEL)
Divine Consolation and Comfort (G)
'One who is a soft landing for your heart'
Archangel ~ CHAMAEL
Libra / Moon (10/9-13)

I AM THAT WHICH...

helps to provide a comforting and supportive atmosphere in which love and enthusiasm for your work, purpose or project might be restored, and where ideas and creativity can flourish without obstacles or discouragement. Since the very nature of all the universes is creative in order to be constantly expanding life, life loves creators and their creations. As an image and likeness of the Divine, you are inherently creative – and we greatly wish you to know that your creative potential is unlimited. 'All you need is love' to feel and experience that truth. While the beginning time of a project is often magical and thrush with enthusiasm and the firing of ideas and momentum, being 'in the trenches' with the 'nitty-gritty' of a project can cause you to lose sight of the big sky of your dream-goal and those initial feelings of inspiration and enthusiasm. Obstacles, detours and waylayers start to show up and soon you feel that you have to work harder and longer, 'leap over tall buildings' and 'run around like a chicken' to keep your vision afloat. However, the truth is that with love and enthusiasm enough, less effort can yield even greater results.

145

The trick is to keep re-enlivening the love that inspired you and the enthusiasm that put your feet on the path. That's where we Angels, and all that is Divine, come in. But since we're already here with and within you, it's more accurate to invite you to come within to us. Here in the sanctuary of your heart, where we offer you the gifts of remembering and restoring you to your inherent divinity, you may tap our power and reinvigorate your entire being. And because beneath all the differences in humankind there is a sameness of heart, you may also receive love and spiritual comfort from each other in your heart-to-heart connections. Beautiful are the times when, even unknowingly, you minister to each other in a moment of need with a kind word or touch, a timely conversation or encounter, a gift of love 'that keeps on giving.'

Dear one, whenever you so desire or need, come unto the warmth and love of the Divine as my YEIAZEL light and be cradled, comforted and restored. And I invite you to draw on my light to magnify yours whenever those in need come for a moment's rest and comfort in the presence of your heart. For your hearts are meant to be soft landings for yourselves and each other, and sacred reminders of the love that birthed you and the love that you are and have always been. Amen...

September 28 – October 5

Angels 41 – 48

Sephira 6

TIPHARETH ~ Beauty, Harmony

Overlighting Archangel

MIKHAEL ~ 'Who is as God'
(Governs with RAPHAEL*) Power and will;
ignites strength, courage and protection for
spiritual seeking and healing

41 **HAHAHEL**

42 **MIKAEL**

43 **VEULIAH**

44 **YELAHIAH**

45 **SEALIAH**

46 **ARIEL**

47 **ASALIAH**

48 **MIHAEL**

* Note that the Archangel correspondences in Sephirot 6 and 8 have been interchanged throughout the centuries by different Kabbalists and schools of thought. After additional research which shows the ways in which both Archangels are active in both Sephirot, I have reversed the primary correspondences presented in the original *Birth Angels* book, but included each as co-governing.

41 HAHAHEL

(HAH-hah-HEL)
Mission (R)
'One who brings Heaven to Earth'
Archangel ~ MIKHAEL (with RAPHAEL)
Libra / Uranus (10/14-18)

I AM THAT WHICH...

helps you to ennoble your chosen work with a sense of higher purpose and the values of Love and Truth that bring as much integrity to the means as the mission itself. One of the questions most often asked by humankind is 'what is my mission, my purpose in life?' We give you this to consider: your mission, 'should you choose to accept it,' is to crack open the light-seeds of love and truth conveyed by your soul into the humus of your heart, and root them in the soil of your own and all of humanity. How you do that is up to you and your unique talents, skills, will and willingness. Often there is a too much referral to the goal, the bottom line and the 'end-game,' while the journey to get there is full of stress, inadequate rest and nutrition and sacrifice of well-being in self and relationships. A student may be in perpetual study cycles of cram and crash. Young lawyers may work all day and night for weeks getting three of four hours of sleep and living on artificial stimulants – as do some creative types in order to 'stay stoked' and not 'lose their edge.' Entrepreneurs may be so constantly 'wheeling and dealing,' 'jumping through hoops' to 'build a new mousetrap' or meet customer demands – that their families for whom they are trying to make a 'better' life never see them.

To the person who is focused on the goal and the bottom line, we say this: most of life's seeming distractions, rest stops, detours, delays, serendipitous happenings and relatings along the way are clues to your true mission. That is because these things reflect HOW you do life, which is often more important than what you do – and which sometimes helps the what to be achieved effortlessly. Like stopping to help a stranger pick up a fallen briefcase as you rush to a business meeting, only to discover that the stranger is the person on the other side of the negotiating table. Like treating all people with respect and kindness, and being hired years later by the janitor you always said hello to who is now CEO of the company you're interviewing with. And then there's the 'ripple effect' – like helping someone with their education who later develops a life-saving cure, or who is instrumental in changing certain laws or policies that will benefit more people. Or the contagious smile that 10 smiles later keeps someone from jumping off a bridge.

These things happen when your heart is fully engaged in life. For thusly, you are living not only the love and truth of yourself, but you are triggering and expanding the love and truth within all you meet. By bringing your inner into the outer world, you are embodying and expressing the Love and Truth of the Heavens upon Earth. So dear one, let my light as HAHAHEL amplify your awareness that your mission is to live fully and lovingly. And though the details are up to you, we will be attending you in the smallest of moments, for truly 'God is in the details' too because there is nowhere or no one that God is not. Amen...

5/2 * 7/16 * **9/29** * 12/10 * 2/18

42 MIKAEL

(MIH-kah-EL)
Political Authority and Order (R)
'One who helps you find your guiding light'
Archangel ~ MIKHAEL (with RAPHAEL)
Libra / Saturn (10/19-23)

I AM THAT WHICH...

helps you to tap the authority of your heart to cultivate your unique talents and aptitudes in order to serve your soul purposes through your work goals, priorities and creations. Despite your seeming subjugation to linear time, humans are not linear but multi-layered. You are not ever dancing to only one melody, but rather an ongoing orchestral medley of awarenesses, considerations, influences, agendas, ideas, thoughts, feelings and actions – each thing with its own 'time signature,' vying continuously for your attention. And as you may ask yourself at times when you feel inundated and overwhelmed, how do you create order in the land? How do you organize your work with the rest of your life so that they are all not out of step with each other?

We suggest that if you order your entire life heart-first, it will all come out all right! When you realize that you are so much greater than the contrived structures of your life plans and business plans, ledgers and bottom lines, you can use your unique talents and aptitudes to expand your chosen work into realms of greater and greater influence and paradigm shifting. This can happen when you understand

151

what we are continually saying in our messages about the 'heart' – that it generates so much more than your feelings and emotions. Your heart is the broadcaster of your soul and as such is the host of your personal truth and the conveyor of particular aspects of Divinity that desire to be expressed within your humanity. As the receptacle of your unlimited soul resources, your heart is the locus for creative inspiration and the 'inner tuitions' that come to you from the eternal realms to form your personal intuitions. Furthermore, your heart holds the power of Divine Love and Truth to alchemize all your worldly knowledge and experience into greater wisdom and understanding. And then there's the 'trickledown effect.' These great attributes of your heart can empower your mind with a more depthful intelligence and the fruits of inspiration that can turn remarkable ideas and innovation into empires of success. Thus, when we suggest for you to be heart-centric in your work place and purpose, you can perhaps understand how useful your heart's resources will be in giving your work the 'edge' it needs to make real headway in the world!

So, inherently heartful and wise one, I invite you to partake of my organizational light as MIKAEL whenever you are temporarily disoriented in 'chicken or egg' dilemmas about what comes first within yourself or any endeavor, project or enterprise. I, and we all angelically will in one way or another, remind you that what comes first is always what matters most when you are thinking with your heart. Amen...

5/3 * **7/17** * **9/30** * 12/11 * 2/19

43 VEULIAH

(vay-OO-lee-AH)
Prosperity (R)
'One who shines the light of possibility'
Archangel ~ MIKHAEL (with RAPHAEL)
Scorpio / Jupiter (10/24-28)

I AM THAT WHICH...

helps you to bring fertility, fruition and largesse to your endeavors without struggle and conflict, and to have a 'knack' for transforming barren or impoverished situations into prosperous and productive scenarios. As we love to remind you again and again, it is the nature of life to continually increase itself through the cyclical movements of contraction and expansion that sustain the ever-expanding flow of all of life. The more you understand lack as simply the natural and temporary ebb in a flow that is always moving toward and through you, the less struggle and misery you will experience during the fluctuations within your life and your endeavors. Everyone welcomes the flow when it is coming to you! It feels wonderful to receive and experience plenitude, and there is an easy sense of gratitude and being blessed in the middle of abundance. However, every flow must have an ebb in order to keep the flow going. So when you resist the pulling back of resources, conditions or circumstances, you are blocking the building of momentum that needs to occur to propel the next new thing on its way to you – and also the space to receive it.

Understanding the principles of ebb and flow can help you to 'go with the flow' without taking the times of ebb personally in a self-recriminating or judgmental way, as if life is punishing you or withholding its blessings. In a world where 'immediate gratification' is king, and where 'quarterly and year-to-year earnings' are expected to continually increase, there is often little appreciation for the importance of the ebb dynamic – and how times of decrease can inspire re-evaluation, the strengthening of certain key areas, and opportunities for creating innovation and new streams of flow. When you take the foggy lens of lack away from your perceptions, you will be better able to see and attune to the natural rhythms of whatever you are endeavoring to create. In doing so, you will come to realize that the thing itself is your partner in its creation, and as long as you are attuning and listening, it will give you the keys to bringing it all the way into being.

I offer you my prosperity light as VEULIAH to help you understand and utilize both ebb and flow – and to become someone who has a knack for turning whatever you engage into a wealth of experience, opportunity and give-and-receive relatings. And lastly, a little 'insider information' on how to turn ebb back into flow and become increased: **invest the bounty of your heart in all you do and be grateful for all that is**. *Thus may your returns be magnified in ever immeasurable ways. Amen...*

5/4 * 7/18 * **10/1** * 12/12 * 2/20

44 YELAHIAH

(yay-LA-hee-YAH)
Karmic Warrior (R)
'One who heals the past by loving it.'
Archangel ~ MIKHAEL (with RAPHAEL)
Scorpio / Mars (10/29-11/2)

I AM THAT WHICH...

helps you to move unencumbered toward the dharma of your soul purposes in this lifetime, so that every new day you may experience the lightness of being fully receptive to the depths of your own being, and be able to share your fullness with others. The more you heal yourself, the more of you is here – and the more you can help others to heal. This is not because you have become a 'master' or a 'high priest' of life (better to continue in the openness of a student!), but because you have 'been there and back' and can use the travails of your own journey to serve as a map and beacon for others. In the hero's journey of the inner warrior, every trial takes the hero into the labyrinth of his own inner unknown in order to transform his burden of harbored wounds and heaviness of spirit into the golden grail of wisdom. On his journey, every outer adversary is a reflection of the adversary within and an opportunity to transform it into an ally. Every trial is a clue to where what he seeks may be found. Every battle won is one that cannot be fought.

As the hero in your own mythic journey, you are not called to vanquish or 'kill off' pieces of yourself to become the 'higher' or 'better' person you want to be – but rather to transform your seeming inner enemies into friends and helpers along the way who each hold the key to the next part of your quest and the clues to where at last your treasure may be found. As the hero within is finally rendered 'naked and undefended' and utterly humbled into surrender, it is then when you may enter into the innermost sanctuary of your heart and be found by that which you are seeking. It is only then when you can know that it is you who are the treasure, and 'the one you have been looking for.'

I wish so deeply for you to see with my YELAHIAH warrior-light that your trials and travails are meant to be the stepping-stones along your journey – not your stumbling blocks. Upon these you may discover the Divinity within your humanity, how to use the way in as the way out, and how to transform nowhere into now-here to see the light of every present moment as the illumination of eternity being revealed to you. As the veils of your past and pre-conceived futures are pulled aside, be unburdened of your self-judgments and become glad for all your experiences. Let each hurt furrow your heart with compassion so that you may pluck the fruit of love for self and others that is now ripe for the harvest at last. Treasure yourself, your longings and your aliveness. Know that what you experience here on this Earth can be experienced only here, and only as the precious multi-faceted diamond that you so uniquely and beautifully are. Dear grail-hearted one, these are the treasures of yourself to which any true quest leads. Amen...

5/5 * 7/19 * **10/2** * 12/13 * 2/21

45 SEALIAH

(say-A-Lee-YAH)
Motivation and Willfulness (S)
'One who fires your heart-motor'
Archangel ~ MIKHAEL (with RAPHAEL)
Scorpio / Sun (11/3-7)

I AM THAT WHICH...

helps to combine your assertive will with its softer expression of willingness, so that the passions and purposes that ignite your outer actions are nurtured and ennobled by receptivity to your emotional and spiritual life and the cultivation of your motivations. As we love to say, it is not just what you do in your life – but how and why you do it. It is easy to get caught up in doing for the sake of doing, keeping on keeping on, showing up day after day, putting in your time. But unless you're also putting your heart and soul into it, the doing will become a pantomime, whatever else it is or could have been. The world will see and be affected by how you do what you do, whether it is with care or with carelessness. And though your personal why may not be something the world needs to know, knowing your own why is central to your determination, courage and passion – and the energy that is transmitted to others in the doing.

When your why is strong, it is not only your reason for doing, but also for being. That is when you know that your why is your purpose. Most intimately, it's between you and yourself, you and the way you jump out of bed in the morning to get to it, you and the reason you hang in there when no one else is giving you the time of day for it, you and your willingness to dedicate your life day after day just to keep doing it. Not because there's any guarantee on the horizon of the world stage, but because it's what gives your heart its own horizon, its every new dawn, its waking dream from which you can never go back to sleep. Imagine being this fired up, this motivated, this moved. This is what happens when the love inside you and your personal why are co-creating – and how you can turn the smallest things into the grandest.

The willingness to keep engaging with your love-fueled why will always refill your secret cache of personal joy, the mystery of who you are that lives in your heart of hearts. And this personal why will also imbue your works with a universal love, truth and power to touch the hearts of others. If acclaim is slow in coming, the willingness to keep returning to the love will keep your heart-fire alive and your will and determination renewed – even if you grow weary at times. And when the world shows its appreciation, that love will still be there for you to return to when the demands of your worldly success would pull you away and afar.

My light as SEALIAH is given to help you be continually receptive to what you love and the great desire of your soul to bring forth love, life and purpose from within you. Together, from within the Divine-Human beingness that you are, we can co-create your heart's desires upon this Earth and renew the infinite love that lives through you, for you and as you...unto others. Amen...

5/6 * 7/20 * **10/3** * 12/14 * 2/22

46 ARIEL

(AH-ree-EL)
Perceiver and Revealer (G)
'One who demystifies the mysteries'
Archangel ~ MIKHAEL (with RAPHAEL)
Scorpio / Venus (11/8-12)

I AM THAT WHICH...

helps you to follow the threads of your feelings and inner truths to reveal which part of the universal tapestry of Divine Love, Thought and Being you are here to uniquely depict through your soul purposes in this life. You have come here to ground a certain constellation of Divine aspects and qualities within human beingness through your specific 'soul agenda.' If you are someone who sees the interconnectedness of all things and the 'bigger picture' in life scenarios and circumstances, it can be challenging to focalize your perception enough to envisage your own piece – your particular identity, place and purpose – in the whole. It may be as if you can see all the changes needed in the world and feel as if you are supposed to orchestrate all of them yourself – and then become paralyzed because 'what can one person do?' In this case, you must take your gaze away from the world and the whole, to see what it is that you have particular feelings and propensities for.

What do you love? What do you find yourself doing when you 'should be' doing something else seemingly more productive? When do you feel most at home in your own skin? What does the small voice within keep trying to tell you in so many different ways? What desire or dream do you keep pushing back down because you assume or fear that it is not practical or doable? If you are unhappy with either success or seeming failure, what is missing? What is the mystery within you longing to be revealed?

Know that for all things on Earth that you might be gifted to perceive, none is so vital and relevant to your time here as perceiving the love and truth of yourself. For if you can truly see yourself (and you can only do so through the lens of love), you will be able to see the wonder of all the universes within the universe of your own being, and know who and why you are here. You will see that you are not here randomly or by chance, but purposefully, by choice and intent. And you will know that above all else, you are here as love, to expand yourself as love through what you do and how you do it, and in doing so, conduct your love energy to all around you that others may be awakened and inspired to the same in themselves, each in their own way.

So, dear self-and-purpose-seeker, wrap the mantle of my ARIEL light around you and fasten it within your heart that you may be revealed to yourself in your true nature as love. Thus may you see that life is not accidental, but the dance of the Divine All particularized through the individuation of love, intention and choice, one timeless heart and soul at a time. Know that 'the one you are looking for is the one looking,' and that with love enough, whatever truth you seek will reveal you in the end. Amen...

5/7 * 7/21 * **10/4** * 12/15 * 2/23

47 ASALIAH

(ah-SA-lee-YAH)
Contemplation (G)
'One who sees the patterns and purposes'
Archangel ~ MIKHAEL (with RAPHAEL)
Scorpio / Mercury (11/13-17)

I AM THAT WHICH...

helps to infuse endeavors with a passion for clarity, truth and the enthusiasm to manifest projects and purposes on the material plane which contain 'hidden' spiritual and symbolic knowledge. When the patterns and interconnectedness of all of life come alive in your seeing and understanding, you begin to vibrate more and more at the energetic levels of unity. You come to realize that seeming separateness is just an individuated expression of the whole, and that nothing in the universe is divided or apart – only multiplied. For the true nature of life is indivisible, and each 'you' and 'I' in existence is as a leaf on one great tree of life, free to twirl about in the wind even as each is rooted and sustained by the umbilical omnipresence of the tree itself.

As these hidden things come to light in your own consciousness, a great joy and enthusiasm may begin to well up within you that cannot be contained. Thus you may be inspired to create works or dynamics of communication and communion that reflect these mysteries of life and which have the power to transmit their inner energies to those who behold and partake of them. Through your work and sharings may you joyfully discover the sacred presence within the shapes and shapeshifting of things, the meanings in metaphors and symbols, the purposes in the patterns, the more whole truths seen through the lens of love, the love that is the cosmic glue between and among all differentiated parts of the whole, the infinite harmonies of the one great universal song, the universal languages that speak to every heart – and thus the sameness of heart underneath your multitude of differences. And in your contemplations, may you come to feel and know that Love is the Divine stem cell carried by every soul, which is longing to proliferate and take root in the heart of every being, every purpose, every endeavor, encounter and relating.

Thus I give unto you my contemplative light as ASALIAH to merge with yours so that you may be confirmed and sustained in your feeling, seeing, doing and sharing. Sing your song truly, dance in step with your own heartbeat, and your love will spill over inward and outward to do unto others what only love can. Amen...

5/8 * 7/22 * **10/5** * 12/16 * 2/24

48 MIHAEL

(MIH-a-EL)
Fertility and Fruitfulness (G)
'One who taps the light-elixirs of life'
Archangel ~ MIKHAEL (with RAPHAEL)
Scorpio / Moon (11/18-22)

I AM THAT WHICH...

helps to fertilize the humus of your humanity with the warming creation light of the Divine so that the light-seeds of your soul may be awakened, nourished and ultimately bear fruit for the ongoing fulfillment of your whole being. As an embodiment of the Divine in a human context, your core soul desire is to make something more of yourself. What that 'more' will be is of your own choosing. Just as with creating anything (or anyone, in terms of reproducing a species), conditions must support fertility and nourishment from the days and moments leading up to conception through the duration of the whole growth cycle. So the questions to consider are – what stimulates the creative juices of your enthusiasm and imagination? What gets you excited and inspires heightened perceptions and sensibilities? What quickens your heart into feeling and intuition, your mind into greater receptivity and awareness, and your body into super-aliveness?

For example, an artist's juices might be stimulated by an afternoon at the museum studying the great works of others, or a ribboned dawn in a breathless span of landscape. A gardener's imagination might be inspired by a visit to a lush botanical garden or a blank canvas of soil that calls for reds and purples. You may be inspired to manifest more of your own love and truth by observing others who are living the joy and expression of theirs. Just as when you intend to 'make a baby,' you must keep yourself nourished, invigorated and amply rested in order to keep the humus of your being conducive to the seeds of ideas and imaginings that have the potential to bring forth new growth in yourself and your creations.

Becoming aware of and acting upon what is needed to stimulate your own fertility is always the first part of creation. In an atmosphere of awareness and full aliveness, the second and third parts emerge naturally – as **attention** to an idea, desire or inspiration becomes focused into **intention**. For the ultimate bearing of fruit, desire must be accompanied by the will to act. Desire (a feeling-preference) is the primordial 'motor' of the universe that drives materialization, and works are the spiritual and material 'children' of desire – and all that are true and life-bearing are propelled by love.

I, MIHAEL, am the fertile love-light of creation given unto you to help your ideas, inspirations and dreams to materialize and proliferate into fruitfulness from your own love-fertilized beingness. In our commingled and co-creative light, go forth and multiply. And may the fruit you bring to harvest be not only nourishing, but seed-bearing for the further bringing forth of the life, love and truth that you are, as that of the Divine manifesting through you for the proliferation of yourself and your fellow beings. Amen...

October 6 – 13

Angels 49 – 56

Sephira 7

NETZACH ~ Victory

Overlighting Archangel

HANIEL ~ 'Grace of God'
Joy, light, insight and true unselfish love
through relationship with the Divine

---

49 VEHUEL

50 DANIEL

51 HAHASIAH

52 IMAMIAH

53 NANAEL

54 NITHAEL

55 MEBAHIAH

56 POYEL

49 VEHUEL

(VAY-hoo-EL)
Elevation, Grandeur (R)
'One who in-spirits the magnificence of the higher'
Archangel ~ HANIEL
Sagittarius / Uranus (11/23-27)

I AM THAT WHICH...

amplifies creative presence and intellectual fire for endeavors motivated by the energies of Love and Truth, which endow you and your creations with the 'super-powers' of **higher consciousness, timelessness and universality.** *Higher consciousness is ascension energy, which, during life, is not about leaving your body but transforming it. By awakening to and tapping your inner resources of* **heart***: love, compassion, intuition and wisdom, and* **soul***: meaning and purpose related to both the cosmic and earthly realms – your body and mind are suffused with greater awareness, and your total being is elevated energetically. Heart and soul qualities vibrate faster because they contain more light – the essential compositional stuff of Divine creation energy. Body and mind qualities contain more earthy and dense vibrations, which are heightened when permeated with the light from the awakened interaction of heart and soul.*

When you create from this higher vibrational energy, you are essentially co-creating with the creation energies of Divine Love, which are limitless. You become able to in-spirit knowing beyond thought, and yet expand the capacity of your mind to form and communicate what you inwardly receive. As your mind becomes aware of its newly endowed powers and capacities, new synapses start firing and it becomes an enhanced conduit and partner with your heart and soul. As you draw from the inherent timelessness of creation energies, your body can take on a visible glow as your physical vibrations are sped up and you become energized. Engaging often at this ascended and inspired level of being and working can actually 'youthify' you if you are also giving your body the nutrition, rest and exercise support it needs to sustain a higher vibratory environment.

The 'perk' of all this is that working at a heart-and-soul-inspired level gives both timelessness and universality to your creations. While there are multitudes of differences in thought, form and expression, there is a sameness of heart and soul across the whole spectrum of humankind in the desire for love, truth, meaning and purpose. While lower-energy thoughts and expressions may be common and pervasive, there are few hearts that do not aspire and quicken to higher possibilities and potentials.

Therefore, dear inwardly and outwardly aspiring one, I offer you my VEHUEL light with which to paint your lofty inner and outer vistas, to climb higher mountains and fly into dreamed-of horizons that truly do await you. And in the meantime, with every next step feel the lighterness of being that comes when you step a little more enthusiastically, a little more lovingly, a little higher and braver! Amen...

5/10 * 7/24 * **10/7** * 12/18 * 2/26

50 DANIEL

(DAH-nee-EL)
Eloquence (R)
'One who uses words to bring forth life'
Archangel ~ HANIEL
Sagittarius / Saturn (11/28-12/2)

I AM THAT WHICH...

helps you to become utterly present and open your heart to 'in-spirit' energies and qualities of the eternal as you speak or write, enabling you to convey wisdom and universal truths to others in a language they can hear and understand. Inspired language and communication is that which bridges the seen and unseen worlds with an all-knowingness from beyond the limitations of time and place, even thought itself – and yet speaks to what is relevant, needed and hoped for in time and place and the innermost longings of the heart. Inspired words are more than eloquent husks of intent. As calls to action, inspired words can convey an omniscient presence to whomever 'has the ears to hear' and the heart to receive so that subsequent actions become ennobled, integritous and capable of uplifting and inspiring all.

True eloquence is not self-conscious. It is an altruistic activity of creation focused on the love-and-truth **essence** *of the invisible other being birthed into words – whether that 'other' is an idea, a vision, or a potential within a person or all of humanity. It is about becoming truly present in a state of loving attunement to that which your words are seeking*

169

to express, even before you know what it is – while also attuning to those who will hear the words, even when you don't know who they are. It involves an 'extraordinary listening' that allows you to hear what hasn't been said, know what longs to be expressed and feel what is needed most in this very moment. In being present with this kind of listening in which you are using love to siphon a more whole truth, you are given words that have the omnipotent power to reveal what needs healing in order to bring forth new life.

Whatever truth you intend to say, love is the message that wants to be heard. Thus, I invite you to draw from and expand my light as DANIEL within you whenever you are writing or speaking so that you may do so from your heart, with your heart, unto the hearts of others. With heart-full attunement to that which wants to be said, you will know that the truth you seek to convey can only be whole in the presence of love. With heart-full communication, you will be able to bring forth that more whole truth by discerning what language, syntax, symbols, associations and timbre of voice will awaken the hearts of your listeners so that they might receive it. So together, dear eloquent one, let us fill pages and podiums with love and truth and the co-creative joy of inspiration! Amen...

5/11 * 7/25 + 26am * **10/8** * 12/19 * 2/27

51 HAHASIAH

(ha-HAH-see-YAH)
Universal Medicine (R)
'One who draws from the Oneness to heal'
Archangel ~ HANIEL
Sagittarius / Jupiter (12/3-7)

I AM THAT WHICH...

helps you to use meaning and purpose in your work-life as a medicinal 'treatment' for cultivating your unique gifts and to feel valuable and valued in your earthly endeavors and contributions. In a meaningful work life, there is a flow of giving and receiving that illuminates the worthwhileness of you, each and all within the whole. Sometimes you do work, social gatherings, spiritual practices or therapeutic modalities hoping to be given something that will uplift you. But all of these are catalysts for calling up what is already within you. Your value, and your cure for all that might ever ail you, is the authenticity, willingness and loving expression of your true self.

The quality of your life and work is determined by how much of your heart you bring to the opportunity or task at hand. You receive value when you bring value – and though you may not be able to name at first the details of your particular value, your authentic and well-intended self is the core value from which all else you might bring and do will unfold. Worry less about the 'what' – and immerse yourself in the 'how.' In one form and way or another, if you sow

171

meaning, you will reap meaning. If you go about your work purposefully, you will realize a sense of purpose and the healing and dignity that comes with that. If you desire to be and feel worthwhile, offer worth while you work. The way in which you work can heal you of hurts which may seem unrelated to the work itself, because it is not as much **what** you do but **how** you do it that adds value and dignity to your experience. If 'what' is the destination, then 'how' is the journey. And it is the 'how' that expands and enlarges you and shows you the more that you are and how much farther you can go than you may have even mapped out for yourself. You may think, or be told, that the purpose is to 'get there' or 'get the job done,' but if the doing is done with meaning, care and regard for yourself and others, then you will have already fulfilled the greater purpose long before the finish line. In this way, there can be no failure, whatever the outcome may appear to be.

I invite you dear one to use my medicinal light as HAHASIAH to illuminate **how** to furrow the fields of your endeavors with meaning and purpose. And if these fields have lain fallow for a time, call on my energy to enliven the Divine nutrients within you to nourish your new seed plantings. Infuse a tired job with new intent, or begin a new work that draws forth the deeper heart of you. Be heart-and-mind-full with every present step in your journey, and the destination will take care of itself – just as the farmer attends to the season at hand, which will yield the season to come in due time. Give your self – your true self – to your work, whatever it may be, and your work will give your self back to you, more true and whole, again and again. Amen...

5/12 * 7/26pm + 27 * **10/9** * 12/20 * 2/28 + 29

52 IMAMIAH

(ee-MAH-mee-YAH)
Expiation of Errors (R)
'One who makes whole'
Archangel ~ HANIEL
Sagittarius / Mars (12/8-12)

I AM THAT WHICH...

helps to course-correct situations that have become compromised and reinstate wholeness as a reference point when 'special interests' of one part of yourself or your work have caused imbalance. The correction of errors is ultimately about re-aligning the parts with the whole. Most mis-takes and mis-directions occur when one aspect, individual or group is acting on its own interests, disregarding the bigger picture and what is needed for well-being of the whole. In work-life this commonly translates as 'short-term gain' at the expense of long-term profit and the well-being of individuals, performance, products and the enterprise itself. Ultimately, what is the profit if you and your business grow fat and rich while you are starving on the inside? Ignoble actions that are justified as 'it's just business' or 'the end justifies the means,' are things you would likely not stand for in your personal life and against those who matter most to you. The damage of 'compartmentalizing' is that the 'sticky stuff' that's been kept boxed into one aspect of your life will sooner or later leak out of the box and contaminate all your other parts and everything and everyone around you.

With all that said, however, in the eternal realms there are no errors – only opportunities for learning how each thing and being are interconnected and affect each other and the underlying reality of the whole. Invite all parts to the party when missions, decisions and bottom-line values are being formed. For entrepreneurs, CEOs and managers, this can mean consulting and collaborating with co-workers, vendors and clients to better understand what is needed for optimum performance at every level. In artistic endeavors, it can mean collaboration between you as the creator, any co-creators and the work itself, as well as a sense of what the audience or client wants. Whatever your work, there must be harmony between your personal self and your work activities and creations so that the wellspring which supplies them, which is you, doesn't dry up.

Dear aspiring one, I invite you to use my light as IMAMIAH to see that the bigger picture of wholeness is born in the heart from the commingling of love, knowledge and experience which yields an intuitive wisdom – and which ultimately comes to live in 'the gut' as 'sheer instinct.' To correct or 'atone' for any 'error' is to bring the prodigal partialities of appetite or desire back unto the whole of the vision, and the whole of you. And so here is the 'bottom line' of our message to you this day: If your pocket rules your business bottom line, you will become far richer if you let it be your 'breast pocket' – the one that is closest to your heart and a sense of true and noble value given and received. Amen...

5/13 * 7/28 * **10/10** * 12/21 * 3/1

53 NANAEL

(NA-na-EL)

Spiritual Communication (R)

'One who sends and receives from within'

Archangel ~ HANIEL

Sagittarius / Sun (12/13-16)

I AM THAT WHICH...

helps you to communicate directly with the originating Spirit of Life, Love and Truth so that you might understand what part of the All you are here to express in this lifetime. We wish you to consider that there is no doctrine, dogma, path, tradition or holy book more potent or relevant to your own unique communication and relationship with the Divine than that which takes place at the altar of your own heart. While external representations and interpretations of spiritual thought and experience, however inspired, can be helpful, comforting, illuminating and uplifting, spiritual communication that is most true and relevant for you is not hearsay. In its most potent form, it is a personal, one-on-one experience, in a language mutually understood, to convey what matters most in that moment. The language that the Divine understands from you is the language of the heart, full with feeling, sincerity and willingness, a language that needs no words – though using words is a way for you to hear what is in the depths of yourself. The language spoken by the Divine to you is the language of Love and Truth which addresses your heart with love, compassion and all-

knowing. It is conveyed through your heart's 'inner tuitions' from that 'still, small voice' within, as well as the encounters, events, coincidences and synchronicities that attend your daily life. Sometimes when your need is great but you are especially 'hard-headed,' your heart may be blasted open with an incoming communication so extraordinary to your life that you are jolted into awakening and listening.

Understanding that you are meant to have personal communion with the Divine is important to understanding that you are here to personally represent, manifest and express particular aspects of the Divine Light and Being in your own human beingness. When the Divine Oneness set into motion its own differentiation through a diverse Creation, your destiny to become a Divine-Human Being became imprinted in the realms of time. Here on Earth we might say that you live the paradox of being Divine on the inside, Human on the outside – an essential soul-oneness expressed into the diversity of physicality. As such, you are here to do things that can only be done on Earth, where the Divine and the Human are commingled into a particularized beingness – things only your particularness can do!

So dear Divinely-empowered unique one, please do draw from my light as NANAEL with heartfelt sincerity to establish 'lines of communication' with the Spirit that brought you forth and continues to sustain you. It will show you which part of Itself you are, as you can show It what more you both can be because of Its presence within you and the tangible reach of your unique humanity. Thus does the Divine Presence become grounded and magnified on Earth! Thus do the wings of Angels unfold in the human heart! And so we say, let there be the light you are, and more! Amen...

5/14 * 7/29 * **10/11** * 12/22 * 3/2

54 NITHAEL

(NIT-ha-EL)
Rejuvenation and Eternal Youth (S)
'One who grows the rose of foreverness within'
Archangel ~ HANIEL
Sagittarius / Venus (12/17-21)

I AM THAT WHICH...

helps to cultivate life-affirming thoughts, feelings and faith in your endeavors by aligning with what you know to be true from within you rather than what seems to be happening to you or around you. A dream, a purpose, a plan, a project all need heart. More than any other part of you, it is your heart's love, energy and enthusiasm that fuels and continually rejuvenates you and your projects, goals and enterprises. With heart you can go the distance of any dream you dare. With heart you can say nay to the nay-sayers and yes to what you know to be true for you, no matter what half-truth or untruth the external world may seem to discourage (un-heart) you with. With heart you can expand the understanding of your mind and the heights of your imagination. With heart, your feet will always find a way, a road, a determination to keep going. With heart, the journey is just as important as the destination. With heart, no horizon, no thing is impossible – even the impossible itself!

All that said, we alert you to the distinction between heart and sheer stubbornness! Heart puts love into motion, whereas stubbornness is the inflexibility of pride. Pride will always hit a wall. Love dissolves walls. Pride can be crushed. Love is fluid and can go around and through any obstacle. Pride is fearful of being found out. Love feels the fear and does it anyway so it can live out loud. Pride is small and always getting smaller. Love is boundless and cannot be measured. It is only when pride dies that your dream has a chance to live. It is only when love is alive that your dream becomes the chance of a lifetime – and your own personal rejuvenator. For as long as you are engaged in creative feeling, thinking and doing, the creative energy which you are siphoning for your endeavors is at the same time re-creating you on the inside – which others can see on the outside of you as a radiance or glow of love-energy and well-being. This is as immediate as how your face lights up by just talking about something you're creating! We love these moments of yours, because we too bask in the glow!

So dear aspiring one, use my eternal light as NANAEL to illuminate, enliven and continually rejuvenate what you love in order to bring it into being and ongoingness. Feed your dream, your ideas, your goals and endeavors with heart-and-soul love. Respect the individuation of your dream and what it wants for itself in the world – for though you are its creator and you will share the same heart, it will have a mind, arms, legs and will of its own. Does that sound familiar? Hear our hearty angelic laughter in the wings!!! And speaking of laughter, bring humor along with your dream so that you don't take the others so seriously when they don't get it. That's okay, they will someday! Or they won't. And then you can just 'take your colors and canvas and go paint where the light is better!' Amen...

5/15 * 7/30 * **10/12** * 12/23 * 3/3

55 MEBAHIAH

(may-BA-hee-YAH)
Intellectual Lucidity (G)
'One who feeds clarity from inner and outer streams'
Archangel ~ HANIEL
Capricorn / Mercury (12/22-26)

I AM THAT WHICH...

helps you to clarify what is most relevant and helpful to your work and purposes from all the options and opportunities available to you, and to measure those against the clear-seeing of who you truly are and what you want. If you are someone who has one particular unmistakable passion, talent or skill, it can be easier to have clarity about what to do with your life – albeit perhaps the part about figuring out where and with whom and what context you want to work in as you develop. However, if you are multi-talented and interested in many areas – and you don't have a staff you can delegate to – narrowing your field of focus enough at certain times to bring forth tangible manifestation can be daunting. You may be able to keep a lot of 'balls in the air' for some time, but at some point you will need to engage one in order to 'hit a homer' – and that may mean you'll have to let the others drop for a bit. In order to do that, you'll need clarity about several things at once – which ball is ready to go the distance, is it a ball that you want to go around the bases for, and is that particular home plate somewhere you really want to be or can it be a stepping stone to take you where you want to be? The only way you can begin to answer these questions is to distinguish among all the options which course of action quickens your energy and excitement and makes you feel most alive in all parts of yourself, starting with your heart.

You are always being bombarded with information and options from both your inner and outer being – both essence and form – soul and body – Divine and Human. Your heart is what bridges these two worlds and teaches them how to talk to and understand each other – and how to choose from the buffet of life to get what all your parts need so that the whole of you is engaged and ultimately fulfilled. Sometimes multi-talented people can become paralyzed into inaction because choosing to do any one thing seems to mean that none of the other things will get done. But when you choose truly, with the greater clarity and scope that the wisdom of your heart brings to your mind, you begin to see that all which needs to be done will get done – and some of it will be effortless.

I, MEBAHIAH, offer my light to help you use your heart-truth, wisdom and intuition as your 'collators' and clarifiers as you research the outer libraries of education, experience and exposure to options, opportunities and catalysts. Thus may you develop clear-seeing about not only where to go and what to do, but all the next steps needed to take you there. Being where you are and doing all you can, with heart and willingness, is the first step in ultimately doing the impossible – which we SO love to be an illuminating angelic party to! Amen...

5/16 * 7/31 * **10/13** * 12/24 * 3/4

56 POYEL

(poi-EL)
Fortune and Support (G)
'One who taps plenitude with feeling'
Archangel ~ HANIEL
Capricorn / Moon (12/27-31)

I AM THAT WHICH...

helps you to use the power to keep 'loving what is' to draw the next thing already on its way to you, which allows resources and support to continue to flow without the impediments of fear and undermining beliefs of lack. If you can truly feel and know that something good is always coming – no matter what package it shows up in – you become an attraction and conduit for that to happen. Feeling is first and central – for true knowing is born out of that. Purpose is generated from feeling, and feeling is what creates quantum possibilities from the seemingly impossible. Mountains become scalable molehills and a low-ceilinged sky gives you the moon on a string. When you bring loving purpose to your work, you are empowering your work to create changes in circumstances and conditions that match the vibration of your feeling – as long as the feeling is **sustained**.

The vibrational energies of life support whatever message you are broadcasting – thus keeping the feeling going that you started with is one of the 'secrets' of success. Strong feeling gets you out of the starting gate and far enough along the path that you 'can't turn back.' And that is usually when the trials come – the day-to-day challenges, delays, distractions, obstacles and setbacks, difficulties and disappointments and assumption of lack that can dull your initial passion and commitment. However, becoming discouraged – losing heart – is what supports and manifests the negative potential of those things. So this is when you have to work your purpose to keep the love alive that initially fueled it – for now **the real challenge is not the success of the work, but the success of keeping your heart in the game, no matter what** – because that's how outer success will come, sooner or later. Just like life. Focus on keeping the faith with a vibrant and steady heart, and all the ducks will keep 'rowing up' – even if a few wander off and a few new ones show up in the process.

I am the POYEL-light in your heart of hearts that can help you to keep the creation energy of love alive so that you keep loving what you do and doing what you love. And while love begets more love, and fear more of itself, please do draw on my light within your heart to realize that fear is just a moment of love forgotten. And so as you journey through your life with an ever-remembering and renewable love, you will have already arrived at your true destination – living a life that restores and sustains love with every loving step you take. That is your true purpose, dear heart, and your true success! Amen....

October 14 – October 21

Angels 57 – 64

Sephira 8

HOD ~ Splendor

Overlighting Archangel

RAPHAEL ~ 'Healer-God'
(Governs with MIKHAEL) Healing,
wholeness, alchemy/transformation,
harmony, awareness.

57 NEMAMIAH

58 YEIALEL

59 HARAHEL

60 MITZRAEL

61 UMABEL

62 IAH-HEL

63 ANAUEL

64 MEHIEL

* Note that the Archangel correspondences in Sephirot 6 and 8 have been interchanged throughout the centuries by different Kabbalists and schools of thought. After additional research which shows the ways in which both Archangels are active in both Sephirot, I have reversed the primary correspondences presented in the original *Birth Angels* book, but included each as co-governing.

57 NEMAMIAH

(neh-MA-mee-YAH)
Discernment (R)
'One who sees through the eyes of the heart'
Archangel ~ RAPHAEL (with MIKHAEL)
Capricorn / Uranus (1/1-5)

I AM THAT WHICH...

*helps you to use your personal heart-truths to discern and cultivate your soul purposes, and to choose work, associations and influences that are compatible with your values and goals. The greatest thing you have come to Earth to do is to love – to **be love**, **share love** and **do love**. Taking on work that allows you to cultivate and practice your purpose is a way to do all three of these at once. The power of doing love is that it uplifts not only your own experience of life and work, but the lives of all you encounter. Some people love their work so loudly and joyfully that they put a smile in the heart of anyone who is graced by their infectious enthusiasm. The mystery within many who have this kind of effect on others is that it is not necessarily the work itself that is their purpose – but the love, care and joy they bring to it – as in the always cheerful 'barista' where you get your perfect morning coffee, or the grocery clerk who takes extra care with breakable items and perhaps even carries the bags to your car – or anyone simply smiling and 'whistling while they work.'*

The details and venues of your own purposes may be grand or humble, complex or simple, and you may do many kinds of work, jobs and career changes throughout your life – but one thing is sure: if you do them with heartfulness, you will be exercising and fulfilling the underlying 'raison d'être' of your purposes. It also helps to facilitate your purposes if you work around healthy and supportive atmospheres and attitudes that are conducive rather than critical or limiting. So, unless your purpose is to come into 'dark' places and be a light for change, it will add to the joy of your process along the way if you work in environments that share and stimulate your values and vision.

My heart-discerning light as NEMAMIAH is given to help you feel and know your soul purposes and how to use them to 'do love' in all kinds of circumstances, whether that means staying or leaving. It is my purpose to help you truly discern and embrace who you are and realize what kinds of environments help you and your purposes to thrive. It does not make you a bigger or more spiritual person to work in a constrictive or low-energy atmosphere, nor to subject yourself to 'lessons' you think you must learn with people and places where you are miserable. You will learn whatever your Divine soul came here to learn – but it is your human right to pick the classrooms and the teachers! Just know this: love is ultimately a greater teacher than pain, though pain can be what opens your heart to receive love. With an open and malleable heart, you can sort through disappointment and forgive outcomes that have not yet been able to materialize. And when understanding is long in coming, with a receptive heart you can feel what there is to feel until you feel your way through it. Amen...

5/18 * 8/2 * **10/15** * 12/26 * 3/6

58 YEIALEL

(YAY-a-LEL)
Mental Force (R)
'One who lightens the heart to empower mind'
Archangel ~ RAPHAEL (with MIKHAEL)
Capricorn / Saturn (1/6-10)

I AM THAT WHICH...

helps to empower your mental capacity and impact by balancing your emotions and drawing from the clarity of your heart-wisdom to bring focus and meaning to your intentions and actions. There is sometimes a fine line between mental strength and stubbornness, mental focus and narrow-sightedness, mental diligence and denial. It is the heart that makes all the difference – and not only your heart-truth that is broadcast from your soul through feelings and intuitions, but how your heart transforms knowledge and experience into a wisdom that informs and gives meaning and purpose to action. Mental force without heart would be like food without flavor, launch without lift, black-and-white without all the juicy colors in between – in short, life without the full spectrum of living, loving and purposing.

For your mental processes to access the resources of insight, intuition and wisdom from your heart, you must be able to distinguish between the feelings and intuitions that act as guidance prompts from your soul and those that are your temporary emotional reactions to life events, circumstances and relatings. These two are different – but

187

sharp and eruptive emotional reactions can be indicators of true feelings not being heeded. **Using your feelings and intuitions as a barometer of what is true or not for you, and allowing them to weigh in on your decisions, is key to formulating mental focus and positive impact on your actions.**

So dear one, this is my light-task as YEIALEL within you – to help you free yourself of the inner and outer conflict of unheeded feelings so that you may be mentally focused, agile and precise. When you sort through the information your feelings are offering and deal with any unresolved hurts or issues, your mind may attain the ballast of peace it needs to advance your purposes without the inner turmoil and impaired clarity that can cloud your thoughts and weaken resolve and results. For as much as your mind likes to think it can operate on its own without your heart as its engine (that's just like a mind now isn't it!), it would likely be just a runaway train of confused thoughts on its own. Bring inner meaning and purpose to every thought and action you undertake – and THAT, my Divine-Human friend who is a heart-soul-mind-body force of reckoning – is full steam ahead and going somewhere! Amen...

5/19 + 20am * 8/3 * **10/16** * 12/27am * 3/7

59 HARAHEL

(HA-ra-HEL)
Intellectual Richness (R)
'One who taps feeling and wisdom to enrich mind'
Archangel ~ RAPHAEL (with MIKHAEL)
Capricorn / Jupiter (1/11-15)

I AM THAT WHICH...

helps to enhance your ability to cultivate a higher intelligence for exploring the patterns and purposes of life, the beauties of diversity and unity within all things and beings, and a desire to share the true treasures of life through your unique perspectives. It has been said by your scientists and philosophers that the mind functions more as an eliminator of information than an accumulator. While this is technically true so as not to have you unceasingly bombarded by the infinite multitude of stimuli from your world and others, it is the applying of meaning to what your mind takes in that makes any of it worth knowing and conducive to you and others. A rich intellect is one that uses the intelligence of your entire being to transform data into relevant knowledge, wisdom and new beingness. There is nothing you may discover with your mind that does not yield more depth in the insight and greater knowing of your heart. And when your heart, mind and soul have truly taken in what you have sought and found, even the vibrations of your physical being can become imbued with a more effective operating intelligence.

The more you come to discern the interconnectedness and underlying unity of all, the more you realize the miracle of life and how each has a place and purpose within the whole. You see that diversity is simply the essential unity of life displaying its many-colored garments and giving the multi-faceted treasures of the inner realms outer voice and vocation, each according to how they are called and what they choose. As you take in more and more of your outer world and come to know what it all means in the context of your own and all of life, you formulate unique perspectives that become your 'message' to the world for your time. And if your understandings and perspectives remain fluid rather than fixed, you will be a Divine-Human repository for the ongoing evolution of love and truth and their infinite combinations – and one whose joy and purpose is to share your perpetual stream of inner wealth with others.

And so dear expanding and expansive one, I join my light as HARAHEL with yours so that we may use our increased light to bring forth that which is timeless to enrich time itself, that which is everywhere to give meaning to place, and that which is truly you to inspire the ever-emerging truths of others. Let us go forth as the many voices of the one and dare to broaden, deepen and heighten all thinking, feeling, being and doing. Amen...

5/20pm + 21 * 8/4 * **10/17** * 12/27pm * 3/8

60 MITZRAEL

(MITS-ra-EL)
Internal Reparation (R)
'One who repairs what is torn'
Archangel ~ RAPHAEL (with MIKHAEL)
Capricorn / Mars (1/16-20)

I AM THAT WHICH...

helps you to become aware of and repair conditions that undermine the success of your work and purposes – and to also see difficulties in your work as a mirror for healing needed in yourself. Most of your life as a Divine-Human being revolves around healing and helping. It is important to understand that the work you choose is a key relationship in your life. Your work has its own inner life, and you and your well-being are part of that. The more you heal your personal self internally, the more whole and healthy your work can become. Likewise, when your creations and works are whole, they transmit and help to sustain wholeness within yourself, and inspire others to their own inner and outer healing and success as well. Because the underlying reality of life is wholeness, all 'holes' that compromise the fabric of wholeness come to the surface sooner or later to be healed. And when they do they usually draw your attention by creating disturbance and chaos, discomfort or disease.

When endeavors and enterprises go through difficult times, it is often because the heart and soul of them have been compromised and sickened – just as with individuals.

If the means betray meaning – whether the end is seemingly noble or not – then integrity is lost. A "sick business" may experience lower yields, seeming setbacks, failures and disappointed expectations, frequent dissension with colleagues and clients and a continual turnover of personnel and vendors. There may be a loss of customers and even loss of the business itself. But these conditions are truly not meant to hurt or defeat you – only to show you where healing is needed, and possible.

Use your own heart to connect with the heart in your work and you will discern what needs healing and how to bring it about. Cleaning out the 'worm in the apple' can be temporarily difficult and unpleasant, but the apple is always worth saving. Following the integritous 'straight and narrow' may take you down a longer road to achieve worldly success, but when it comes it will be solid, life-affirming and inspiring to you, your work and others.

Thus, dear apple of my Divine Eye, wrap the cloak of my healing light around your personal hurts and let them be healed, and take that healing into your work so that it may have the power to compound wholeness within you and all who engage with it. For your deepest soul desire is to bring your fellow beings the treasures of your heart-and-soul purpose that you may encourage and help to inspire their own true desires and beautiful possibilities. Amen...

5/22 * 8/5 * **10/18** * 12/28 * 3/9

61 UMABEL

(OO-ma-BEL)
Affinity and Friendship (R)
'One who thrums the threads of interconnectedness'
Archangel ~ RAPHAEL (with MIKHAEL)
Aquarius / Sun (1/21-25)

I AM THAT WHICH...

helps you to use the heart-energy of affinity to draw to you whatever you desire, and then to sustain the flow by sustaining your feeling for it and drawing others to you with similar affinities so that your collective purposes may be shared and increased. Creating affinity is the first step to fulfillment and is at the core of a great universal law, which is that things and beings of similar resonance are drawn to each other. To draw friendship, become a friend. To draw love, be loving. To create a better and truer world, be a better and truer individual. To create the fulfillment of your dreams, hold the vibration of them inside you. To accomplish your soul purposes, be at one with them, take them into your heart and feel them until you become them. For it is your heart, with all its feeling, wisdom-making and unlimited access to the Divine, that is able to love-into-being whatever you truly want and attract co-creators also working with love, vision and noble intent.

As those who work in the arts especially know, it is the energies of affinity which help the creator and that which wants to be created to find and fulfill each other. Through

193

the affinity of inspiration and co-creation, the inner finds its outer expressions – colors find their canvas, song finds a voice, feelings find words and essence finds form. All creations are made of love, and love is the great shape-shifter – flowing from within to take any outer form that you so desire to bring forth. This is how any and every purpose finds its time and place in the world, whatever kind of dreamer and doer you are in whatever field of endeavor.

So today, dear one, partake of my UMABEL affinity-light to hold in your heart a feeling for that which you desire. Do not ask for it or bemoan not having it and thinking or fearing that you lack it. Simply imagine its presence in the universe of energies around you and see and feel it coming into your life to be with and within you and all around you. Be present with it, attuning to it, conversing with it, loving and listening to how it wants to take form and be born through you. Be full of gratitude and joy for its presence, feeling how fully you believe in it, feeling that it too believes in you. And thusly dear creator one, it shall come – for it was already within, waiting for your love to bring it the rest of the way here. And know especially that 'wherever two or more are gathered' with affinity and friendship in the name of love and noble intent, there shall be given a creation that is greater than the sum of its creators. Amen...

5/23 * 8/6 * **10/19** * 12/29 * 3/10

62 IAH-HEL

(EE-a-HEL)
Desire to Know (R)
'One who calls you to the unknown'
Archangel ~ RAPHAEL (with MIKHAEL)
Aquarius / Venus (1/26-30)

I AM THAT WHICH...

gives you the urge for 'the road less traveled' to make the unknown knowable and the undone doable, and to 'travel light' in your knowledge-gathering journeys in order to have room for lightness of being and taking life itself more lightly. Your inner and outer journeys are always reflections of each other. The more you have ventured into your own inner unknown, the more knowable the outer unknowns become. And the less you allow the dramas of life to entrap you in brambles of self-judgment and resistance, the more flow, fun and success your journeys will have. It takes both courage and a sense of adventure to take on the unknown and to innovate new ideas and doings. While your destination is what puts you on the path – your soul-goal is the journey itself and the possibility to manifest gifts and talents that perhaps you didn't even know you had. And maybe even some new friends!

When you see everything in your path as stepping stones rather than stumbling blocks, all your obstacles both inner and outer will become opportunities. Thus you may be vastly enriched way before you arrive at any kind of 'destination *success' that is measureable monetarily. For example, it may be your goal to collaborate on a project with a colleague which will require a lot of research, discussion and co-creating. While the structure of the work and the shared goal may be your focus, the deeper content of your work is what you discover and catalyze about yourselves and each other, as well as coming to understand the deeper nature – or the soul – of the work itself. The deeper purpose of work is always to come to know and understand more about yourself AND the work – and to grow, expand and ennoble both. If you keep to that truth, then you will not find yourself in work that has become a 'petty tyrant' in your life, undermining and debilitating to both your own potential and the work itself.*

I invite you to partake of my IAH-HEL light to experience all this and more · – and especially to come to know how to make your work more effortless by infusing great feeling into your desire to know. For that which you want to know also wants to be known, and attending to it with your love and presence will cause it to hasten to you. As in the mystery of 'be still and know that I am,' allow yourself moments to pause between your doings for the respites of daydreaming, contemplation, rest, play and pleasure, and feeling rather than thinking – moments when you are not striving or seeking. For often these are the moments when what you desire to know is simply given. And that is because in your lighter times, there is less in the way of your simply receiving. And so dear one, give some moments to yourself and your work when you are able to receive the greatest gifts of knowing – earned not by doing, but by being. Amen...

5/24 * 8/7 * **10/20** * 12/30 * 3/11

63 ANAUEL

(a-NA-oo-EL)
Perception of Unity (S)
'One who sees the Oneness within the many'
Archangel ~ RAPHAEL (with MIKHAEL)
Aquarius / Mercury (1/31-2/4)

I AM THAT WHICH...

helps you to see the bigger picture of your purpose and how all the parts and pieces must work together to create the whole and give it the power to transmit wholeness. In Earth life, wholeness is composed of its parts, and each 'unit' of wholeness has a purpose and potential to contribute to or detract from group wholeness. This is how the human body and being works – as a collaboration of the biological components that result in your outer physical structure with the intangible aspects of heart, mind and soul that compose your inner being. As you bring your individual wholeness to others through work and relatings of all kinds, you help to create the wholeness of groups, communities and nations. However, when there is a breakdown in the wholeness of the individual components, it ripples out so that the greater wholeness is compromised, which in turn contaminates the individual parts further. If this is prolonged, awareness of the underlying reality of unity which gives meaning and purpose to all the parts is lost. But even in the case of egregious groups and organizations, one cannot heal the whole without healing the individuals that compose it first.

*So coming back to you and the parts that compose you –
your heart is the hub for all the different spokes of your own
being and your relatedness to other beings – and the wheel
of your life needs the contributions of all your parts to move
you forward. While each part is clamoring for meaning and
sovereignty at times, it cannot be found in separateness-
consciousness or at the expense of each other. If you
undertake purpose with one part and neglect or disrespect
the other parts, your purpose will be weakened and only
partially realized. This is what happens when you deplete
your body or mind with overwork or you leave your heart
out of your work. Or when the contributions of others are
devalued or disregarded. Or when you create great
innovative or inspiring works, but do not allow those works
to instruct and inspire you to live and love in the greaterness
of your own potential – and thereby the greater potential of
all humankind. But when all the parts are employed with
respect, appreciation and enthusiasm – then what you
create is greater than the sum of the parts – a whole whose
meaning is not divided by the parts, but multiplied.*

So dear you who are an **individual** *– an* **indivisible**
*entity whose wholeness is greater than any sum of parts, yet
dependent on those parts to be whole – let my light as
ANAUEL help you to see the whole that enlivens your parts,
and the parts which compose your whole. And let my light
expand within your heart so that love, intuition and wisdom
will awaken purpose within each part that it may be justified
and fulfilled within the whole. Thus what you bring in co-
creation with and for all the parts of the world will be the
ever-ongoing transmission of unity. Amen...*

5/25 * 8/8 * **10/21** * 12/31 * 3/12

64 MEHIEL

(MAY-hee-EL)
Vivification (Invigorate & Enliven) (G)
'One who brings the elixir of life to the vessel'
Archangel ~ RAPHAEL (with MIKHAEL)
Aquarius / Moon (2/5-9)

I AM THAT WHICH...

helps to combine intellect (knowledge), heart (enthusiasm) and commitment (will) to work together in order to quicken ideas and innovation into a material reality that has the power to transmit life-affirming energies. Knowledge is particular information from your personal 'data-base,' experience and the world-at-large which your mind has acquired and 'downloaded' as relevant to your interests. Enthusiasm is born in the heart from Spirit and carries the potential of your power as a Divine-Human being. The power of the word is understood in its syllables: 'En + theos + asm' = the ecstasy of being 'with God' – as you say 'with child' – meaning that you are pregnant with creation energy. Enthusiasm brings forth creation energy – which is simply love – to transform knowledge into the wisdom and intuition that directs your will into action.

Enthusiasm is what brings the juiciness of inspiration and flow to any endeavor, project, purpose or plan. Intellect and will without the passionate lifeblood of heart would be an attempt to force creation rather than being a co-creator and vessel for it. When you allow your heart to be the heart in whatever you do, then whatever you create will have a life and lifeblood of its own to sustain itself and transmit its life-giving energies way beyond the time and place of its birth, beyond the you as you knew yourself to be before that moment of creation.

As the most attuned gardeners know, there is a point in every growing cycle – after seeds are lovingly planted and watered and the rich soil and warmth begin their mysteries of nourishment – when you must leave off your strivings and let the hidden life within the seed siphon the power and potency it needs to come into fruition in its own due time. For life inherently brings forth more life from whatsoever you seed. And as it does, it most surely and sweetly brings forth new life within you as well.

As the fading light of yesterday is renewed by today's dawn, may you go forth with renewed heart to turn each step into a quantum leap and each leap into a new horizon in the sky of your dreams. Feel my life-breathing light as MEHIEL expand within you to fill your heart and the heart of your creations. Go forth pregnant 'with God' and multiply the indivisible wholeness of a wholehearted life that has the infinite power to harvest itself in the bringing forth of new life. Amen...

October 22 – 29

Angels 65 – 72

Sephira 9
YESOD ~ Foundation

Overlighting Archangel
GABRIEL ~ 'God is my Strength'
Guidance, vision, inspiration for faith
and connection to the Divine; vessel for
giving and receiving, creative fertility,
and the ebb and flow of life's seasons

---

65 DAMABIAH
66 MANAKEL
67 EYAEL
68 HABUHIAH
69 ROCHEL
70 JABAMIAH
71 HAIYAEL
72 MUMIAH

65 DAMABIAH

(da-MA-bee-YAH)
Fountain of Wisdom (R)
'One who brings the ocean to the river'
Archangel ~ GABRIEL
Aquarius / Uranus (2/10-14)

I AM THAT WHICH...

stimulates the flow of your 'inner gold' of wisdom to spill over into your external world as the rare treasures of your heart which enrichen your unique endeavors and creations. True purpose does not ask of you selflessness, but **selfness** *– to bring yourself into fullness with your unique passions, talents and gifts in order to cultivate the potential greaterness of your existence and to help inspire and uplift the existence of others. Your heart is your treasure, for it gives voice to the aspirations of your soul and supplies the enthusiasm, wisdom and courage for earthly manifestation of your soul purposes. Thus your offering to the world becomes not a sacrifice, but a fulfillment.*

Your sciences and psychologies have long regarded the mind as the 'master organ' of your being, though new technologies are suggesting otherwise. We will say only that as the seen and unseen worlds are allowed to more and more cooperate together in search of life's greater truths, both your scientific and spiritual realms of understanding will have greater potency and power. For now, bridges are built through your arts, and your hearts! The mysteries and creations of the heart are far more powerful in their cause and effect on your whole being. It is your heart that has the power to siphon the greater knowings that form your intuitions. It is your heart whose feelings and emotions help to navigate you through the world with truth and meaning. It is your heart which receives every thought, idea and experience you bring to it with compassion and understanding. It is your heart which has the ability to transform knowledge and experience into wisdom with the all-seeing, all-knowing power of love. Thus it is your heart which holds the keys to your soul-purposes on Earth. For only your heart can amplify your human experience with your Divine soul-identity so that you might bring the full treasure of your humanity into being and expression.

Wisdom cannot be acquired – it is made and cultivated in the heart. Wisdom is what happens when you bring knowledge and experience to your heart to be commingled and transformed with love into greater understanding. Wisdom uses the parts to form a greater whole. Because of love, wisdom is a more whole truth and is not fixed, dogmatic or rule-making. The holistic nature of wisdom is fluid and kinetic so that it can flow to any part of you at any moment where greater feeling, knowing and understanding of the whole are needed.

Thus dear one I, DAMABIAH, invite you to tap your inner font of wisdom and drink the light-elixir of wholeness that together we distill within your heart so that you may know and feel how to disperse the unique treasures of yourself unto the world. Amen...

5/27 * 8/10 * **10/23** * 1/2 * 3/14

66 MANAKEL

(MA-na -KEL)
Knowledge of Good and Evil (R)
'One who lights a candle to cure the darkness'
Archangel ~ GABRIEL
Aquarius / Saturn (2/15-19)

I AM THAT WHICH...

helps to use the darkening of a waning season as a period of gestation, deepening awareness and the re-gathering of energies in preparation for the seeding of new light, life and the expansion of dreams, ideas and endeavors. In the cultivating of soul purposes in the humus of your being and life, there will be seasons of flow and seasons of ebb which are life's natural contrasting expressions of positive/light and negative/dark energies. Do not resist or fight the times of ebb, but draw on the love and truth within your heart to illuminate their messages. Thereby the presence of light may be expanded, and the darker times will dissipate and leave you with lessons learned and resiliency strengthened. In your work-life, the knowledge of 'good and evil' is about knowing if the work you do expands or diminishes the light and truth of yourself and your higher purposes. It is about knowing what matters most, where your loyalties and allegiances are, and where your heart stands when your back is to the wall.

There is nothing you can take with you when you leave this Earth except love, and nothing you can leave behind that has lasting and regenerative value except love. In all change, the only constant is the energy of love which has the power to bring life into being. Where there is loss of business, a client or a job, do not focus on the loss but rather the opportunity to review and renew. Even in the face of financial challenge, keep your personal resonance positive and use your love and the gift of time and space to go toward work that is more expressive of your heart's calling. You do not lose anything in life that truly belongs to you at the soul level, and the loss of material forms can remind you of the things and people in your life that have truer, greater value – as when a family home and possessions are lost in a fire or flood, but the family itself is unharmed. You may lose your job or business – but you do not lose yourself, your experience, skill, knowledge or the love you put into it. Love is the eternal compositional stuff of life that animates forms and matter – and when forms fade or change, it is the love that remains and is here for you to reclaim. Thus, there is no loss of 'things' that cannot be healed and replenished – in one form or another – by the bottomless flow of light and love that the heart is able to siphon from the realm of the eternal.

And so, dear Divine-Human one who on Earth must ride the tides of ebb and flow that are natural to this plane, use my light as MANAKEL to take these tides less personally and to put your attention and energy into what you want to increase and 'bring to light.' Have faith that while the dark does have its times of encroachment, the nature of the universe is that of light ever-expanding. Align yourself with this understanding and you too will expand as an emissary and co-creator of that same universal light that also shines in your very personal heart. Amen...

5/28 * 8/11 * **10/24** * 1/3 * 3/15

67 EYAEL

(AY-ya -EL)
Transformation to the Sublime (R)
'One who illumines the inner star'
Archangel ~ GABRIEL
Pisces / Jupiter (2/20-24)

I AM THAT WHICH...

helps to light, lighten and enlighten your way in the face of adversity, and to use the making of matter as opportunities to accumulate more and more light in the well of your heart and in the expression of your soul purposes. Your soul comes to Earth to do great things, humble things, healing and helping things – and at the heart of them all its greatest desire to do true and loving things. Of course, in human life things can happen 'on the way to the forum' that cause noble soul intent to be forgotten, muffled and derailed. This is why the Divine Heart has given you the Angelic aspects and light-allies of itself to dwell within and endow your 'earth-heart' with feeling, inspiration and inner tuitions to awaken your soul-memory and purposes so that you might bring these into the denser vibrations of your human parts.

When you consider your purposes in life and how to express those through your work, know that you are not here to live for the care and upliftment of others while sublimating your own care and healing. You are not here to do work that depresses and debilitates you in order to put food on the table and a roof over the heads of you and your loved ones. You are not here to 'sacrifice' yourself for any person or cause, but to come into personal fulfillment so that you may bring the greater treasure of yourself to the world – the love that lives within you that is given to others through your presence – and which keeps on giving when you have 'left the building.' Life is about rooting Divine Love and Truth on Earth and helping them to branch out from heart to heart across the planet. Thus may your lives, your beings and your endeavors be fashioned around a cooperation between matter and meaning in which matter is used to broadcast and proliferate meaning.

So, dear meaning-seeking one, I EYAEL, am the 'light stores' within you from which you may always draw to amplify and strengthen your inner and outer resources. I am here to lighten your heavy lifting and lift you to higher ground when you are inundated by challenge and difficulty. When you are caught in the undertow of your life's natural ebb and flow, look to the light I am shining as a beacon from the shores of your heart. When your days feel like moonless nights, reach beyond your 'low-ceilinged skies' to the eternal light that brought you here, and know that there is no end to what truly matters. Do not do battle with darkness, but rather let there be light – and all meaning and matter will be illumined and transformation will begin. Amen...

5/29 * 8/12 * **10/25** * 1/4 * 3/16

68 HABUHIAH

(ha-BU-hee-YAH)
Healing (R)
'One who loves hurt into healing'
Archangel ~ GABRIEL
Pisces / Mars (2/25-29)

I AM THAT WHICH...

helps you to use the creation energy of love to heal the disturbances and dysfunctions in your work life, as well as their reflections in yourself. The thing that connects you and whatever work you do is the meaning and purpose you bring to it. Just like you, when your work is cut off from meaning and purpose it can become focused on quantity of productivity for maximum short-term gain, while the core slowly becomes 'rupted' – ruptured and weakened through the compromise of quality and integrity. It can be difficult to see at first that your work is intrinsically sick if it is producing volume because volume of production and income is a desired value in the business world. So the first symptoms of something being 'off' may be more discernible in you and your co-workers. Stress, fatigue, a sense of unease, emptiness and frequent illness are all symptoms of working in a sick business.

One of the most common and insidious forms of sickness in a business is when the value system of the business undermines the personal values of the employees. If you have an active work-life, you probably spend at least half of

209

your waking life working, so truly your well-being is affected when you have one set of values in your personal life and another in your work-life. You may try to compartmentalize the different parts of your life and yourself, but the boxes will inevitably leak into each other because in the underlying reality of unity, everything is a part, a reflection and a cause and effect of everything else.

So the task then is to purify and strengthen the core – the heart – by giving it voice and purpose within you, your colleagues and the work itself. The more heart you bring to your work and awaken in yourself, the more creation energy you bring forth. Creation energy is the quantum presence of love. What we mean by 'quantum presence' is the nature and power of love to be everywhere at once bringing forth new life – in both the seen and unseen worlds, in temporal and eternal time, in the heart of the universe and in everything and everyone. In a healthy and thriving business this means a "global" integrity, enthusiasm and creative collaboration in a shared mission with meaning throughout all aspects of the business, which includes an atmosphere that is conducive to the well-being of employees, even if you are the only employee.

Thus, dear healer and 'healee' – I offer you my HABUHIAH light to heal the core of your work and your life by infusing both with the meaning and purpose only the heart and soul can bring. Love yourself, love your work, love your life and each other into more noble beingness – and all will come into fulfillment as it should. Amen...

5/30 * 8/13 * **10/26** * 1/5 * 3/17

69 ROCHEL

(ro-SHEL)
Restitution (R)
'One who brings back your lost parts'
Archangel ~ GABRIEL
Pisces / Sun (3/1-5)

I AM THAT WHICH...

helps to restore what seems to be lost or missing in order for you to have the more fulfilled experience of living you know deep down you should be having. For all the different qualities of the Divine that all the different beings in creation express, each of you express something unique that is a particular 'constellation' of Divine and Human beingness. Throughout your lives you are given inner and outer prompts and clues to help quicken your soul memory in order to know what you are here to do through the vehicle and experience of this life. When you lose conscious connection with your soul and its Divine 'power supply' that conducts the currents of meaning and purpose through your heart longings, loves and truths, the flow of cosmic energy can weaken and your life may begin to lose its spark. This can easily happen when the challenges and demands of your world overshadow the infinite possibilities always waiting below the surface of everything, and most relevantly, the surface of you. So when you feel you've lost something, look beneath your emotional reactions to find true feeling for what you love – not just what is familiar and comforting.

Look into your heart to see your innermost longings and what is natural and compelling to you. Look behind the masks of all outer conditions and appearances. Here in the "underneath" places are the clues to help you find anything you seem to be missing in your experience of life.

Thus, if your work has lost its luster – or never had it – and your time spent doing it feels hollow and unsatisfying, then you must look beneath the surface of both yourself and your work to see that they are missing the same thing – meaning and purpose. Your work may be lackluster because it's missing you – your whole meaningful and purposeful self. Or perhaps your personal meaning and purpose is different than that of the work you do. If that is the case, then there is simply a disconnect between the two and likely you need to find or create work that is more in alignment with the greater love and truth of yourself.

Thus, dear one, I offer you my light as ROCHEL to help restore your awareness of the Divine that resides within your soul as the eternal power supply of your greater being and doing on Earth. Whenever you feel that something is lost or missing in your life and your work, shine our shared light into all your inner nooks and crannies. Look for outer signs and clues, pay attention to where you are led, listen to the whispers of dreams and feelings and best friends for what is too close to see without a reflection. And when you find what you are looking for, take it to heart and it will surely, lovingly and truly find you back. Amen...

5/31 * 8/14 * **10/27** * 1/6 * 3/18

70 JABAMIAH

(ya-BA-mee-YAH)
Alchemy (Transformation) (R)
'One who turns base mettle into gold'
Archangel ~ GABRIEL
Pisces / Venus (3/6-10)

I AM THAT WHICH...

helps to purify and ennoble all aspects of your human beingness so that the highest creation forces, which hold the hologram for your wholeness, may be received and used for extraordinary healing, renewal and the expression of your true self and soul purposes in your life and work. As we never tire of saying, Love does not want you to 'get out of the way' to bring something higher through you, but rather to become the way. You are not here to eschew the flesh or banish the ego or suppress 'unruly' thoughts, desires and feelings, nor are you here to be some idealized notion of perfection. The only perfection which is possible and spiritually 'advantageous' for you to achieve on earth is your own trueness. There is no formula in the world for that, except the one that is distilled in the cauldron of your own heart when you bring it the 'raw materials' of your humanity and allow the love and truth therein to transform your base mettle into gold. In this rarer light of your sacred heart, you can finally see the magnitude of who you are and what you are here to do with your Divinely-endowed human beingness.

And so, may you experience the fullest, bravest most outrageously wonderful life that you imagine for yourself in your heart of hearts and soul-longing. For we wish you to understand this about your work and purpose here: Whatever and however many tangible creations you bring forth, mountains you move or good deeds and accolades you accumulate, the only thing you can take with you when you leave this planet is what your soul can carry. And that is the love and lightness of true being with which you have lived your life and given the treasures of your heart and higher-mind unto others. Therefore, dearest one, my transforming light as JABAMIAH is given unto you so that your inner gold may be wrought within and brought from your heart into all the precious parts of you, and also unto the world that it may carry on your light-legacy of love and truth ever manifesting. Amen...

6/1 * 8/15 * **10/28** * 1/7 * 3/19

71 HAIYAEL

(HA-ee-ya-EL)
Divine Warrior & Weaponry (R)
'One who wins the battle that cannot be fought'
Archangel ~ GABRIEL
Pisces / Mercury (3/11-15)

I AM THAT WHICH...

helps you to infuse your work and purpose with win-win scenarios of integrity and success for all involved, and to increase creation energies by keeping the focus on supporting what you want to achieve rather than fighting against potential underminers. In any endeavor, taking a stand on higher ground means to not engage in the moment-to-moment skirmishes and low-lying areas where wars are fought, but not won. And instead, being willing to formulate a treaty – a solution – in which possibilities for all are expanded instead of limited. Higher ground in all your negotiations involves an understanding of the eventual goal. If you want to have friendly, fair and equitable relationships for ongoing business activities, then all parties must be listening to what each other's needs and desires are. A business that heeds what everyone needs, and at the same time makes room for accommodations that are agreeable to all, is much more equipped to succeed than a scenario of 'every man for himself.'

A particular area of vulnerability for a business is competition. If a competitor is trying to 'steal' a client or defame your good name, to do battle with him by defaming him back or stealing one of his clients is to 'stoop' to his level, thus doing battle in his home territory where he has the advantage. Rather, if you support your own clients with honor, integrity, effective and innovative services and products, you will ultimately win the war without engaging in the battle – even if you lose a few short-sighted clients along the way. Or, say you are a candidate in a political election who declines to engage in political slander, rather maintaining your integrity and focus on a positive agenda. While you may lose an election or two (or not), over time you will build trust and amass a constituency based on your character and consistency of positive and solution-based words and actions. There are many ways to give your heart to the world – you don't need to win elections to win in life.

*What all this is saying dear light-warrior, is to not engage with energies that de-enliven and darken your purposes. No matter how noble a battle or cause may seem, as soon as you begin to fight either for or against it, you have become contaminated by the verb itself, for you, like your opponent, are fighting. So I, HAIYAEL, suggest to you to replace the 'F' in 'fight' with the **love-and-life-affirming 'L'** of **light**, the better to see by and win the war that cannot be fought. Your best defense is always to just be the light of a loving truth. So carry your own home territory of higher ground wherever you go, and shine. Those drawn to the light will be drawn to you and your work and endeavors. Those who are drawn to the dark will sooner or later realize they are fighting something that they have no weapons against, and they will flee, or join you! So whatever you do, wherever you go, just shine, shine, shine on. Amen...*

6/2 * 8/16 * **10/29** * 1/8 * 3/20

72 MUMIAH

(MOO-mee-YAH)
Endings and Rebirth (R)
'One who uses endings to begin again'
Archangel ~ GABRIEL
Pisces / Moon (3/16-20)

I AM THAT WHICH...

helps you to 'leaf' the past behind in order to seed vitality for new creations by allowing a time of rest and gestation so that nutrients and energies can be re-gathered for rebirth and renewal in due time. Endings are vehicles for change. While you and your purposes and creations are expanded and evolved through change, there is a part of you that wants things and people to remain the same. But like a baby about to be born, there are times when you must leave a womb-like familiarity in order to take on greater life and growth. Endings and beginnings are sacred passages of ebb and flow that occur in all aspects of your life, and it is our joy to be especially active with and within you during these times to help steward your way through the call for renewal – for these are the times when you have the potential to make quantum leaps in awareness and new beingness.

In the evolution of your purposes, your job and job titles and tasks may change from time to time. These changes may signal the need or opportunity for a new way of working, a new infusion of purpose, a reevaluation of bottom lines, values and goals, and so on. Some of the changes may be

217

welcome, and some you may resist. Sometimes the ending of a job or aspect of your work may come without a new beginning immediately 'on its heels' or 'on the horizon.' While that uncertainty can be uncomfortable, time is giving you the gift of a pause – a bridge between an end and a new beginning that you call a 'transition' – so that past experiences can be assimilated and composted into new energies for seeds that are just taking root. The transitional processes of dormancy and gestation are often invisible, and you may feel a sense of loss or lack of control as if you or your business are at a 'stalemate' or 'neither here nor there.' But if you use this time of transition for review and the cultivation of new ideas and innovations rather than resisting, worrying, judging or blaming, then you will hasten the coming of what will be and the new potentials and opportunities that renewal always brings with it.

So dear changing and evolving one, I invite you to expand my MUMIAH light in your heart so that you might courageously attune to your new gifts-in-the-making and begin to love into being what will be, even before you know what that is. And especially use this time as an opportunity to revisit your personal and work purposes and their compatibility with each other. If they are at odds or even a little off-track, this is a good time to re-align and repurpose. And know dear one that in our own Angelic way, we are 'breathless' at every ending in your life because of the great potential for you to increase your light and life by the new choices you make. Feel us around and within you, and know that we are here to help you bounce a little as you hit ground and give you loft as you get ready to launch the next thing. Godspeed to you – in your own perfect timing! Amen...

Amen...Amen...Amen

Here end the daily Angel wisdoms for this cycle of time as we have again moved through Nine of the Ten Sephirot on the Tree of Life. In the Tree of Life symbology Sephira 10 is a "bridge" realm leading from the Angelic Heavens to Earth, the realm of saints and ascended souls. Therefore, there are no Angels (except Archangels) correspondent to this last Sephira of the Tree. However, it is included here in order to complete the spiritual descent of the Heavenly Tree of Life unto Earth so that it may take root and branch out within the hearts of all humanity.

.

Sephira 10

MALKUTH (SHEKINAH)

Relates to the Kingdom of Creation

and the Realm of Saints and Ascended Souls

Overlighting Archangel

SANDALPHON and METATRON

These two Archangels, sometimes referred to as "spiritual brothers," are arguably said to be the only two Archangels who were once human and taken up to the heavens without having experienced human death: METATRON as Enoch, and Sandalphon as ELIJAH. Metatron's unmanifested creation energies in KETHER are finally manifest in MALKUTH and the SHEKINAH (feminine aspect of the Divine) which gives birth to Earth. Thus here METATRON is the link between the Divine and all of humanity. SANDALPHON is the overlighting Archangel of the Earth itself – planetary "caretaker" who grounds Divine Love within humanity and our relationship with the natural world in order to cultivate higher consciousness on Earth.

TERAH COX

Appendix I
Your Personal Birth Angels

The ancient mysteries reveal that our souls come to Earth for many lifetimes in order to heal the unhealed hurts and issues that occur in human life, which we call our "karma," so that we might advance the "dharma" of our soul purposes in service to the expansion of the Divine within ourselves and others. Because of the density and forgetfulness of Earth-life, it is said that in our choosing of circumstances for each lifetime we also choose certain influences, guides and cosmic aspects around our time of birth that will act as symbols or "signatures" to remind us what we came here to do. Similarly, the 72 Angels reveal that through their hierarchies of relationship to Creation and time, we also are "assigned" – or choose – a constellation of particular Angelic Energies to dwell with and within us whose qualities of Divine love-and-light-consciousness correspond to our soul purposes and challenges for this lifetime. While a kind of hologram of all 72 Angels are imprinted within us, we are especially attended by the three Angels that were the supporting energies at the moment we were born, who throughout our lives help to quicken and amplify the spark of Divinity carried within our soul and its expression in time, meaning and matter. Our Birth Angels take on these roles as they work with the physical, emotional and mental aspects of our being:

Your **Incarnation Angel** ~ Expresses qualities of the Divine Being and Will through human physical existence, will and life purpose. Corresponds to your five-day period of birth and the qualities, challenges and expressions of your physical being and purpose.

Your **Heart Angel** ~ Expresses qualities of Divine Love through the feelings and wisdoms of the human heart. Corresponds to your actual day of birth, your emotional qualities, challenges and potentials, and supports the cultivation of inner truth, wisdom and love for self and others.

Your **Intellect Angel** ~ Expresses qualities of Divine Mind through the constructs and creations of human intelligence.

Corresponds to your time of birth (within 20 minutes), your mental qualities, challenges and potentials and the cultivation of greater awareness and higher-mind. Those born at a cusp time (on the hour or 20 minutes before or after) have two Intellect Angels (for a total of four Birth Angels). (See p. 215 to discover your Intellect Angel(s).)

You can know who your Birth Angels are by corresponding your day and time of birth to the Angels' days and times of influence. (See below, as well as *The 72 Angels of the Tree of Life* quick-reference chart at www.terahcox.com/birth-angels.html). I would like to clarify the use of the terms "govern," "influence" and "support." The Angels are spoken of as governing certain days and times, as well as the different planes of human beingness (physical, emotional and mental). What is meant by the term governing here is *influence, correspondence* and *support*. Ideally, because of our Divinely-endowed birthright of free will, we humans govern ourselves and support each other (an arguable concept!). The Angels, therefore, are not within and among us to govern us, but to bring a positive influence of Divine energies and support for our highest good – which is to amplify and magnify the truth of who we each uniquely are and support the fruition of our soul purposes and potentials in time and eternity.

The 72 Angels' Days of Incarnation Support

Your Incarnation Angel expresses the Divine Being and Will in human physical existence, will and life purpose. Their dates of governing correspond to the five-day period around your birth and the qualities, challenges and expressions of your physical being and purpose.

3/21 - 25	1 VEHUIAH – Will & New Beginnings
3/26 - 30	2 JELIEL – Love & Wisdom
3/31 – 4/4	3 SITAEL – Construction of Worlds
4/5 – 9	4 ELEMIAH – Divine Power
4/10 – 14	5 MAHASIAH – Rectification
4/15 – 20	6 LELAHEL – Light of Understanding
4/21 – 25	7 ACHAIAH – Patience

4/26 – 30	| 8	CAHETEL – Divine Blessings
5/1 – 5	| 9	HAZIEL – Divine Mercy & Forgiveness
5/6 – 10	| 10	ALADIAH – Divine Grace
5/11 – 15	| 11	LAUVIAH – Victory
5/16 – 20	| 12	HAHAIAH – Refuge/Shelter
5/21 – 25	| 13	YEZALEL – Fidelity, Loyalty, Allegiance
5/26 – 31	| 14	MEBAHEL – Truth, Liberty, Justice
6/1 – 5	| 15	HARIEL – Purification
6/6 – 10	| 16	HAKAMIAH – Loyalty
6/11 – 15	| 17	LAVIAH – Revelation
6/16 – 21	| 18	CALIEL – Justice
6/22 – 26	| 19	LEUVIAH – Expansive Intelligence, Fruition
6/27 – 7/1	| 20	PAHALIAH – Redemption
7/2 – 6	| 21	NELCHAEL – Ardent Desire to Learn
7/7 – 11	| 22	YEIAYEL – Fame/Renown
7/12 – 16	| 23	MELAHEL – Healing Capacity
7/17 – 22	| 24	HAHEUIAH – Protection
7/23 – 27	| 25	NITH-HAIAH – Spiritual Wisdom & Magic
7/28 – 8/1	| 26	HAAIAH – Political Science & Ambition
8/2 – 6	| 27	YERATEL – Propagation of the Light
8/7 – 12	| 28	SEHEIAH – Longevity
8/13 – 17	| 29	REIYEL – Liberation
8/18 – 22	| 30	OMAEL – Fertility, Multiplicity
8/23 – 28	| 31	LECABEL – Intellectual Talent
8/29 – 9/2	| 32	VASARIAH – Clemency & Equilibrium
9/3 – 7	| 33	YEHUIAH – Subordination to Higher Order
9/8 – 12	| 34	LEHAHIAH – Obedience
9/13 – 17	| 35	CHAVAKIAH – Reconciliation
9/18 – 23	| 36	MENADEL – Inner/Outer Work
9/24 – 28	| 37	ANIEL – Breaking the Circle
9/29 – 10/3	| 38	HAAMIAH – Ritual & Ceremony
10/4 – 8	| 39	REHAEL – Filial Submission
10/9 – 13	| 40	YEIAZEL – Divine Consolation & Comfort
10/14 – 18	| 41	HAHAHEL – Mission
10/19 – 23	| 42	MIKAEL – Political Authority & Order
10/24 – 28	| 43	VEULIAH – Prosperity
10/29 – 11/2	| 44	YELAHIAH – Karmic Warrior
11/3 – 7	| 45	SEALIAH – Motivation & Willfulness

11/8 – 12	46 ARIEL – Perceiver & Revealer
11/13 – 17	47 ASALIAH – Contemplation
11/18 – 22	48 MIHAEL – Fertility & Fruitfulness
11/23 – 27	49 VEHUEL – Elevation & Grandeur
11/28 – 12/2	50 DANIEL – Eloquence
12/3 – 7	51 HAHASIAH – Universal Medicine
12/8 – 12	52 IMAMIAH – Expiation of Errors
12/13 – 16	53 NANAEL – Spiritual Communication
12/17 – 21	54 NITHAEL – Rejuvenation & Eternal Youth
12/22 – 26	55 MEBAHIAH – Intellectual Lucidity
12/27 – 1/31	56 POYEL – Fortune & Support
1/1 – 5	57 NEMAMIAH – Discernment
1/6 – 10	58 YEIALEL – Mental Force
1/11 – 15	59 HARAHEL – Intellectual Richness
1/16 – 20	60 MITZRAEL – Internal Reparation
1/21 – 25	61 UMABEL – Affinity & Friendship
1/26 – 30	62 IAH– HEL – Desire to Know
1/31 – 2/4	63 ANAUEL – Perception of Unity
2/5 – 9	64 MEHIEL – Vivification (Invigorate/Enliven)
2/10 – 14	65 DAMABIAH – Fountain of Wisdom
2/15 – 19	66 MANAKEL – Knowledge of Good & Evil
2/20 – 24	67 EYAEL – Transformation to Sublime
2/25 – 29	68 HABUHIAH – Healing
3/1 – 5	69 ROCHEL – Restitution
3/6 – 10	70 JABAMIAH – Alchemy (Transformation)
3/11 – 15	71 HAIYAEL – Divine Warrior & Weaponry
3/16 – 20	72 MUMIAH – Endings & Rebirth

The 72 Angels' Times of Intellect Support

The following shows all 72 Angels in their one 20-minute period in the 24-hour day when they are governing the intellect plane, and thus expressing particular qualities of Divine Mind in your human intellect to help you cultivate awareness and higher-mind. Your Intellect Angel is the one that was governing 20 minutes within your time of birth. Thus, if you were born at 12:10 a.m., your Intellect Angel would be 1 VEHUIAH. Those born at a cusp time – on the hour or 20 minutes before or after – have two Intellect Angels; so if you were born at 12:20, your two Intellect Angels would be 1 VEHUIAH and 2 JELIEL. Note that because we are met by the Divine wherever we are, your Intellect Angel will be the one that was governing at the time and place you were born.

Midnight (a.m.) to Midday (p.m.)

12:00 – 12:20	1 VEHUIAH – Will & New Beginnings
12:20 – 12:40	2 JELIEL – Love & Wisdom
12:40 – 1:00	3 SITAEL – Construction of Worlds
1:00 – 1:20	4 ELEMIAH – Divine Power
1:20 – 1:40	5 MAHASIAH – Rectification
1:40 – 2:00	6 LELAHEL – Light of Understanding
2:00 – 2:20	7 ACHAIAH – Patience
2:20 – 2:40	8 CAHETEL – Divine Blessings
2:40 – 3:00	9 HAZIEL – Divine Mercy & Forgiveness
3:00 – 3:20	10 ALADIAH – Divine Grace
3:20 – 3:40	11 LAUVIAH – Victory
3:40 – 4:00	12 HAHAIAH – Refuge/Shelter
4:00 – 4:20	13 YEZALEL – Fidelity, Loyalty, Allegiance
4:20 – 4:40	14 MEBAHEL – Truth, Liberty, Justice
4:40 – 5:00	15 HARIEL – Purification
5:00 – 5:20	16 HAKAMIAH – Loyalty
5:20 – 5:40	17 LAVIAH – Revelation
5:40 – 6:00	18 CALIEL – Justice
6:00 – 6:20	19 LEUVIAH – Expansive Intelligence, Fruition
6:20 – 6:40	20 PAHALIAH – Redemption
6:40 – 7:00	21 NELCHAEL – Ardent Desire to Learn
7:00 – 7:20	22 YEIAYEL – Fame/Renown

7:20 – 7:40	23	MELAHEL – Healing Capacity
7:40 – 8:00	24	HAHEUIAH – Protection
8:00 – 8:20	25	NITH-HAIAH – Spiritual Wisdom & Magic
8:20 – 8:40	26	HAAIAH – Political Science & Ambition
8:40 – 9:00	27	YERATEL – Propagation of the Light
9:00 – 9:20	28	SEHEIAH – Longevity
9:20 – 9:40	29	REIYEL – Liberation
9:40 – 10:00	30	OMAEL – Fertility, Multiplicity
10:00 – 10:20	31	LECABEL – Intellectual Talent
10:20 – 10:40	32	VASARIAH – Clemency & Equilibrium
10:40 – 11:00	33	YEHUIAH – Subordination to Higher Order
11:00 – 11:20	34	LEHAHIAH – Obedience
11:20 – 11:40	35	CHAVAKIAH – Reconciliation
11:40 – 12:00	36	MENADEL – Inner/Outer Work

Midday (p.m.) to Midnight (a.m.)

12:00 – 12:20	37	ANIEL – Breaking the Circle
12:20 – 12:40	38	HAAMIAH – Ritual & Ceremony
12:40 – 1:00	39	REHAEL – Filial Submission
1:00 – 1:20	40	YEIAZEL – Divine Consolation & Comfort
1:20 – 1:40	41	HAHAHEL – Mission
1:40 – 2:00	42	MIKAEL – Political Authority & Order
2:00 – 2:20	43	VEULIAH – Prosperity
2:20 – 2:40	44	YELAHIAH – Karmic Warrior
2:40 – 3:00	45	SEALIAH – Motivation & Willfulness
3:00 – 3:20	46	ARIEL – Perceiver & Revealer
3:20 – 3:40	47	ASALIAH – Contemplation
3:40 – 4:00	48	MIHAEL – Fertility & Fruitfulness
4:00 – 4:20	49	VEHUEL – Elevation & Grandeur
4:20 – 4:40	50	DANIEL – Eloquence
4:40 – 5:00	51	HAHASIAH – Universal Medicine
5:00 – 5:20	52	IMAMIAH – Expiation of Errors
5:20 – 5:40	53	NANAEL – Spiritual Communication
5:40 – 6:00	54	NITHAEL – Rejuvenation & Eternal Youth
6:00 – 6:20	55	MEBAHIAH – Intellectual Lucidity
6:20 – 6:40	56	POYEL – Fortune & Support
6:40 – 7:00	57	NEMAMIAH – Discernment

7:00 – 7:20	58 YEIALEL – Mental Force
7:20 – 7:40	59 HARAHEL – Intellectual Richness
7:40 – 8:00	60 MITZRAEL – Internal Reparation
8:00 – 8:20	61 UMABEL – Affinity & Friendship
8:20 – 8:40	62 IAH– HEL – Desire to Know
8:40 – 9:00	63 ANAUEL – Perception of Unity
9:00 – 9:20	64 MEHIEL – Vivification (Invigorate/Enliven)
9:20 – 9:40	65 DAMABIAH – Fountain of Wisdom
9:40 – 10:00	66 MANAKEL – Knowledge of Good & Evil
10:00 – 10:20	67 EYAEL – Transformation to Sublime
10:20 – 10:40	68 HABUHIAH – Healing
10:40 – 11:00	69 ROCHEL – Restitution
11:00 – 11:20	70 JABAMIAH – Alchemy (Transformation)
11:20 – 11:40	71 HAIYAEL – Divine Warrior & Weaponry
11:40 – 12:00	72 MUMIAH – Endings & Rebirth

Appendix II

A Brief Summary of the 72 Angels Tradition

My first **Birth Angels** book in 2004 introduces the tradition of the 72 Angels of the Tree of Life which was said to have been systematized beginning in the 12th century by Rabbi Isaac the Blind in France, and carried forward into 13th-15th century Gerona, Spain by Rabbis, scholars and mystics working within the **Judaic Kabbalah** and other mystical traditions. I list the important influences here to give some philosophical backdrop to the Angel wisdoms: **Christian Gnosticism** (direct knowing of God through personal communion), **Sufism** (coming closer to God while still in life through love and unity-identification), **Neoplatonism** (espousing the "One" and the "Infinite" beyond being, from which all Life is brought forth containing the essence of the Divine One) and **Hermetics** (the Egyptian and Greek spiritual alchemy of transforming base *mettle* into the gold of wisdom and ennobled beingness in order to manifest Heaven on Earth). These spiritual pioneers of the Middle Ages and Renaissance believed in the basic right of all humankind – both men and women of all creeds and cultures – to have direct communion with the Divine without the dictates or exclusivity of dogma. Heretical notions for the time!

In the 13th century, a yeshiva in Gerona, Spain was founded by Talmudist and Kabbalist Rabbi Moses ben Nachman (Nachmanides), who was a disciple of Kabbalist Azriel of Girona, who himself was a disciple of Isaac the Blind. In 1492 the school and Jewish grotto were walled up and abandoned during the Conversion/Expulsion Edict of the Spanish Inquisition and remained hidden until excavations began in the 1970's of the area, now referred to as "the Call." The manuscripts that were found dealing with the 72 Angels and Tree of Life tradition are said to reveal a vibrant creation cosmology which adds more Angelic detail to the ancient symbology of the Tree as a universal "flow chart" for the descent and differentiation of the Divine Oneness into the hierarchies of the 72 Angels and all of Creation. Working with the Tree of Life as a prototype for universal man, these 12th-15th century

Kabbalists understood the 72 Angels as key "connectors" in the mysteries of the Divine-Human two-way relationship. As the "edible fruits" of the Tree given to humanity for ingesting the Divine and quickening our own soul essence, the Angels enable the Divine to branch out into Earth through the soul-heart-mind-body of human beingness, and the Human to return to our Divine roots inwardly through transformation and ascendance back up the Angelic Tree into higher consciousness.

People are often surprised to learn that there is no one definitive Kabbalah holy book or text. The Kabbalah was for centuries a mystical oral tradition that was practiced within, but somewhat hidden from, mainstream Judaism. It is largely based on esoteric study of ancient wisdoms, revelations, inspired texts and inner receivings passed down through the ages from Rabbis, mystics and scholars to the next generation of disciples and students. The earliest known Kabbalah work, arguably attributed to Abraham or Moses, is the *Sepher Yetzirah* ("Book of Formation"), a short but intense mystical treatise about how the utterances of the first "Creator Sounds," which ultimately became known as the Hebrew Alphabet, brought about Creation. It is the cosmology in this ancient work that Kabbalists through the ages have referred to in their understanding of the nature of the Divine and Creation.

Birth Angels referenced Kabbalistic and multi-traditional sources spanning over 2500 years, as well as certain works by French mystic and scholar François Bernad-Termes, writing as Haziel, whose numerous books dealing with the Kabbalah, Angels and astrology drew from the excavated manuscripts. I was introduced to the 72 Angels tradition around 1996-97 by French Canadian and Swiss-French teachers Kaya and Christiane Muller, who work with the 72 Angels and dream symbology (www.ucm.ca/en/info/the-72-angels). Also, after *Birth Angels* was published in 2004, A.S.I.A.C.T., a color education institute associated with Aura-Soma Colour-Care Products in the U.K., developed a series of courses under the guidance of Chairman Mike Booth relating the 72 Angels and the Tree of Life to their color products and philosophies.

The 72 Angels tradition is compelling because there is a kind of spiritual science and ageless but exacting wisdom to it that calls us to an Angel-assisted practice of inner engagement through feeling and direct knowing rather than adherence to a particular religion or dogma. While the tradition does not espouse or exclude religion, it has the capacity to re-enliven any religion or path since it contains aspects that are in the mystical hearts of most, if not all, traditions. The foundational premise of the 72 Angels and Tree of Life tradition is that God is within us and we are within God, and both the Divine and the Human are evolving and expanding together. Perhaps most significant is that it answers some of the deepest longings and potentials we hold in our individual hearts, where the Angels do their transformational work.

Below is a brief recap of my understanding and inner experiences of the central aspects of the tradition that invite us to look at the Angels, and ourselves, in a whole new light.

The 72 Angels as the Divine within the Human

The 72 Angels are understood by Kabbalists working with the Tree of Life symbology as energetic expressions of the 72 Names, Being and Qualities of the Divine. While some thinking regards the hierarchies of Angels as created beings, the Angelic Tree of Life mysteries say that the 72 Angels are the initial *emanations* of the Divine Itself, revealing and energetically embodying the great diversity of Its nature. This is likely a correspondence to what some Judeo-Christian literatures call "Angels of the Presence" which came forth on the "first day" and were said to represent the faces of God, as God Itself.

In addition, as "birth-gifts" of qualities of the Divine Essence acting from within and among us, the 72 Angels illuminate and amplify the vast spectrum of possibilities and purposes within humanity, while our personal Birth Angels especially signify and support what we each are here to do, heal, express and manifest in our current lifetime. To summarize, these are the special roles of the Angels in our human lives:

As angles and amplifiers of light-consciousness, they magnify those qualities of the Divine which they embody and which our soul has chosen to manifest in our current lifetime through our physical, emotional and mental being and purpose.

As transformers of our base mettle into a goldenness of being, they help to heal the karma of harbored hurts and issues so that we may be free to express the dharma of our soul purposes in service to ourselves, each other and the Divine.

As conveyors of the Love and Truth which compose the totality of the Divine Nature, they help to create a bridge between soul and body by amplifying our soul-voice and purposes within our hearts through love, compassion, intuition, heart-truth and wisdom.

As two way messengers between the Human and the Divine, they are not just carrying prayers and answers back and forth. They are transmitting Divine Essence and Energies into us, and returning what we experience in our human Earth-life to the Divine. This two-way exchange evolves and expands both the Divine and the Human.

As expressions of the diverse nature of the Divine, the Angels illuminate for us the diversity of qualities which compose our own Divine-Human nature, as well as help us to understand that *it takes the totality of humankind and the beings and things of the natural world and beyond to reveal and express the diverse nature of God*. This suggests the importance of not just tolerating each other's diversities, but embracing ourselves and all beings, ways and things as valuable and illuminating pieces of the bigger picture puzzle of the Divine and Life Itself. Truly, we are each here to literally "flesh out" our part of the picture with the fullness of our unique being – for ourselves, each other and the fullness of the Divine on Earth.

* * *

For more detail about the 72 Angels tradition, see *Birth Angels ~ Fulfilling Your Life Purpose with the 72 Angels of the Kabbalah* and Vol. 1 of *Birth Angels Book of Days*. (TerahCox.com & Amazon.com)

BIRTH ANGELS BOOK OF DAYS

Daily Wisdoms with the 72 Angels of the Tree of Life

Volume 1: March 21 – June 2
Relationship with the Divine

Volume 2: June 3 – August 16
Relationship with Self

Volume 3: August 17 – October 29
Relationship with Work and Purpose

Volume 4: October 30 – January 8
Relationship with Others

Volume 5: January 9 – March 20
Relationship with Community and the World

Additional Offerings
Quick-Reference Charts: The Kabbalistic Tree of Life
72 Angels of the Tree of Life ~ Days & Hours of Governing
Birth Angels Prayer & Meditation Cards
Speaking, Coaching & Workshops
www.TerahCox.com

---

*You are invited to share your experiences
in working with the 72 Angels
by contacting the author at*
HeavenandEarthWorks@gmail.com

About the Author

TERAH COX has worked with the Kabbalah, Christianity, Sufism and other spiritual traditions and wisdoms throughout her life in exploration of the common threads of Love and Truth in their mystical hearts. She is the author of *The Story of Love & Truth, Birth Angels ~ Fulfilling Your Life Purpose with the 72 Angels of the Kabbalah, You Can Write Song Lyrics*, the five-volume series of *Birth Angels Book of Days* and several works in progress. She is also a speaker and coach on the subjects of individuation and life purposing, creativity, diversity/unity and spirituality.

Formerly a writer for the Aura-Soma Colour-Care-System® in the U.K., she was also signed to the music publishing companies of Columbia Pictures, BMG Music (U.S. and Scandinavia), Warner-Chappell and various European music publishers as a lyric writer of over 150 songs recorded for CDs, film and television. Her poetry-art designs for greeting cards, prints and more are online and in galleries and retail shops across the U.S.

* * *

Books, speaking, coaching and workshops
www.TerahCox.com

Original greeting cards, prints, word-art & books
www.HeavenandEarthWorks.com

E-Cards with original music, messages and art
www.MilestonesConnect.com

Printed in Great Britain
by Amazon.co.uk, Ltd.,
Marston Gate.